American Teaching about Russia

American Teaching about Russia

CYRIL E. BLACK
JOHN M. THOMPSON
Editors

Indiana University Press
Bloomington

Contents

List of Tables

Contributors

CYRIL E. BLACK is professor of history at Princeton University. He served as chairman of the subcommittee of the Joint Committee on Slavic Studies, appointed by the American Council of Learned Societies and the Social Science Research Council, which planned the appraisal of Russian studies in the United States of which this volume is a part.

ROBERT F. BYRNES is chairman of the Department of History and director of the Russian and East European Institute at Indiana University. His publications include: *Bibliography of American Publications on East Central Europe, 1945-1957*, and (ed.) *The Non-Western Areas in Undergraduate Education in Indiana*.

GEORGE BARR CARSON, JR., is director of the Service Center for Teachers of History of the American Historical Association. He is the author of *Electoral Practices in the U.S.S.R.*

JOHN M. THOMPSON is a lecturer in history at Indiana University. As a member of the staff of the Social Science Research Council from 1957 to 1959, he administered the appraisal of Russian studies in the United States of which this volume is a part.

American Teaching about Russia

Introduction

THE EVENTS of the Second World War and its aftermath brought the Soviet Union to the forefront of international affairs and turned American attention to that part of the world. In the succeeding years the desire of Americans to know more about Russia and the Soviet system has increased, and the study of Russia in the United States has expanded at a rapid rate. In 1956, as the first decade of postwar growth in this field drew to a close, those concerned with the state of Russian studies became convinced that a review of the record and some organized reconsideration of problems and opportunities would be beneficial. As a result, a general survey and appraisal of the position of Russian studies in the United States was initiated in the spring of 1957 under the auspices of the Joint Committee on Slavic Studies, a body of scholars engaged in teaching and research relating to Russia and Eastern Europe appointed jointly by the American Council of Learned Societies and the Social Science Research Council.

This appraisal was in charge of a Subcommittee on the Review of Russian Studies,[1] which set for itself the following objectives: in the light of the experience of the decade since the war and in view of changing educational and

1. The members of the Subcommittee on the Review of Russian Studies were Cyril E. Black (Princeton University), chairman; Robert F. Byrnes (Indiana University); Charles Jelavich (University of California at Berkeley); Henry L. Roberts (Columbia University); Marshall D.

13

world conditions, to survey and assess the achievements and problems of Russian studies in the United States; and to suggest fruitful lines for its development in the next decade. Six major aspects of Russian studies were examined: research; library resources; the professional organization of those concerned with the study of Russia; and graduate, undergraduate, and secondary education relating to Russia. Eleven papers by individual scholars dealing with research on Russia in various disciplines, originally prepared at the request of the Subcommittee on the Review of Russian Studies, have been published.[2] Library resources and needs were analyzed in a separate but complementary survey undertaken by the Committee on Slavic and East European Studies of the Association of Research Libraries.[3] Problems of professional organization in Russian studies were examined and discussed, and proposals in this regard are now under consideration by the Joint Committee on Slavic Studies and others interested in this question. The present volume gives the results of the appraisal

---

Shulman (Harvard University); Donald W. Treadgold (University of Washington); and Melville J. Ruggles (Council on Library Resources). The Review was administered by John M. Thompson (Social Science Research Council). A summary of its findings has been published in "An Appraisal of Russian Studies in the United States," *American Slavic and East European Review,* XVIII (October, 1959), 417-41.

2. *American Research on Russia,* edited by Harold H. Fisher, with an introduction by Philip E. Mosely (Bloomington: Indiana University Press, 1959).

3. The results of this study are being published in Melville J. Ruggles and Vaclav Mostecky, *Russian and East European Publications in Libraries of the United States* (Bloomington: Indiana University Publications, Slavic and East European Series, Vol. XX, 1959).

14

of the role of Russian studies in graduate, undergraduate, and secondary education in the United States.

When this appraisal was undertaken, two important and relatively new factors affecting Russian studies were the opening of the Soviet Union to brief visits by tourists and scholars, and widespread public concern to know more about Russia. During the past two years, contacts with the Soviet Union and public interest in the area have grown rapidly and have become major influences on the future of Russian studies in the United States. An American-Soviet cultural exchange agreement was signed early in 1958, and seventeen Soviet and twenty-two American graduate students were exchanged in the academic year 1958-59. The launching of the Soviet satellites in the fall of 1957 led to increased national concern with study of the Soviet area and contributed in part to the passage of the National Defense Education Act, with its provisions for strengthening foreign area and language training, including Russian.

II

One of the central purposes of this appraisal was to stimulate widespread thought and discussion concerning the problems and prospects of the study of Russia in American education in the years ahead. In keeping with this purpose, a number of conferences were held. The first such conference dealt with graduate education on Russia and met in New York City on December 6-7, 1957. At this conference the members of the Joint Committee on Slavic

15

Studies, along with other scholars and administrators concerned with Russian studies, discussed an early draft of Chapter 1. This draft was based on an intensive study of the record and problems in this field, following visits to the leading institutions concerned with the study of Russia. A revised draft was discussed at another conference held in Berkeley, California, on March 29-30, 1958. This meeting was attended by some seventy scholars and administrators from a dozen institutions on the West Coast of the United States and Canada.

Since it was manifestly impossible to examine the way in which the study of Russia was carried on in all colleges and secondary schools, two different selective studies were made at these levels. In examining undergraduate education, the state of Indiana was chosen as a roughly representative state, and a pilot study was made of the attention devoted to Russia and other non-Western areas in undergraduate education in Indiana. Eastern Europe, Asia, and Africa, as well as Russia, were included in order to ascertain how the position of Russian studies compared with that of these other areas frequently neglected in American education.

In the late spring of 1958 every college and university in Indiana was visited. A draft report based on the results of this intensive survey, as well as several working papers on such specific problems as curriculum, language instruction, and extracurricular activity, was then discussed at a conference in Bloomington, Indiana, on September 18-20, 1958. This conference was sponsored jointly by the American Council of Learned Societies, Indiana University, and the Joint Committee on Slavic Studies, and was attended by

16

over sixty representatives of the colleges and universities of Indiana and by representatives of other institutions and scholarly organizations. Great interest in the development of non-Western studies in undergraduate education was evidenced, and many fruitful ideas were presented and discussed. The final paper on undergraduate education, included as Chapter 2 of this volume, is based on the Indiana survey and the Bloomington conference.

A slightly different procedure was adopted for the appraisal of the role of Russian studies in secondary education. In this field, a pilot study did not seem to be the best approach. Instead, approximately twenty teachers, principals, administrators, textbook editors, and other leaders in secondary education were invited to meet with a small number of scholars in Russian studies to examine the problems involved in developing the study of Russia in secondary schools. This conference was held in Washington, D. C., on October 17-19, 1958, under the sponsorship of the National Association of Secondary-School Principals, the American Council of Learned Societies, and the Joint Committee on Slavic Studies. It discussed several working papers dealing with problems of content and curriculum in Russian studies in secondary education, and with instruction in the Russian language and teacher education. Chapter 3 of this volume is a distillation of the findings of this conference.

III

Those engaged in Russian studies in the postwar years have faced a number of problems. For almost a decade one of the severest handicaps for the study of Russia was the lack of contact with or access to the Soviet Union as a result of restrictions on travel and exchange of persons and materials imposed by the Soviet government. In addition, for several years in the middle of this period, American acquisition of Soviet publications was curtailed by customs restrictions of the United States government. These factors, in addition to Soviet reluctance to make available much fundamental data, hampered research efforts; scholars had to base their studies on scant materials and on information indirectly acquired or constructed. At the same time, the inaccessibility of the Soviet Union removed an important dimension of graduate education in Russian studies and forced heavy reliance on intensive methods of area training. Though there could be no real substitute for first-hand experience in Russia, this handicap was compensated for, by dint of imagination and hard work, as effectively as the circumstances permitted.

The partial opening of the Soviet Union to travel by Americans and the development of exchanges with some groups in Soviet life present important challenges and opportunities for Russian studies in the United States.[4] Such contacts should benefit graduate education and research on Russia particularly, although all aspects of Russian studies will derive advantage from this new phase in Soviet-

4. A paper on this subject, originally prepared as an address to a conference on research sponsored by the Joint Committee on Slavic Studies in conjunction with the tenth anniversary celebration of the Russian Research Center of Harvard University, January, 1958, has been published: Henry L. Roberts, "Exchanging Scholars with the Soviet Union," Columbia University *Forum*, I (Spring, 1958), 28-32.

American relations. It is already clear that more accurate information concerning the Soviet Union and a clearer comprehension of differences and similarities in the Soviet and American ways of life will be among the results.

Another major problem was the scarcity in 1946 of the basic resources necessary for the development of Russian studies—scholars and teachers, research materials, and books and teaching aids. To extend the personnel resources of the field, maximum use was made of the relatively few specialists already trained, with many scholars having to double as advisers, planners, administrators, and government consultants. At the same time a new generation of scholars and teachers was rapidly trained. In some disciplines, such as sociology and geography, where only a few individuals had been concerned with problems of the Russian area, a small but significant number of additional scholars were educated, fresh approaches were devised, and new research was published. In these and such other disciplines as education, philosophy, fine arts, and the history and sociology of science, however, there are still only a handful of American scholars studying Russian developments.

Library and research materials were collected through the combined efforts of the Library of Congress and university libraries, with the assistance of the Joint Committee on Slavic Studies. In addition, such special projects as the Harvard Refugee Interview Project and the Research Program on the U.S.S.R. of the East European Fund drew upon the knowledge of former Soviet citizens and scholars to add significantly to our store of information concerning

Soviet society. A number of excellent studies of various aspects of Russian and Soviet society were written, basic treatises and new textbooks were published, and projects to provide teaching aids of various kinds were completed or are now under way. Several important translation programs were undertaken, and the *Current Digest of the Soviet Press*, sponsored by the Joint Committee on Slavic Studies, took its place as an invaluable aid to students, teachers, scholars, journalists, and many others interested in following Soviet affairs. As a result of these measures, materials on Russia in English are now available in much greater quantity than they were ten years ago. The various efforts such as those described above, as well as the significant advances in graduate education, benefited very greatly, both in financial support and in initiative and planning, from the early and continuing interest of the Carnegie Corporation of New York, the Ford Foundation, and the Rockefeller Foundation.

A measure of the considerable success with which the field of Russian studies overcame the difficulties facing it in the postwar decade is its accomplishments in graduate education on Russia and its achievements in research. In 1946 both the universities and the government urgently needed highly skilled personnel and mature scholarship concerning the Soviet Union. The main effort in Russian studies during the postwar years was therefore concentrated on meeting these immediate needs, and relatively little emphasis was placed on a possible role for Russian studies in undergraduate and secondary education in the United States.

20

Similarly, no particular effort was made to transmit to the informed public the findings of the scholarly world concerning Russia, although several universities sponsored brief institutes or special summer programs on Russia and a number of individual scholars participated generously in forums, radio and television programs, and lecture series designed for this purpose. In addition, a few practicing journalists received Russian area training, and a small number of students educated in Russian studies embarked on careers in the communications field or in organizations dedicated to improving public understanding of international and foreign affairs.

The papers that follow should be read with this background in mind. They reflect the intention of those concerned with Russian studies to maintain and strengthen graduate education and research on Russia, as well as their increasing interest in presenting the findings of American and other Western scholarship with regard to Tsarist and Soviet Russia to undergraduates and secondary-school students and to the American public in general.

1

Graduate Study of Russia

CYRIL E. BLACK & JOHN M. THOMPSON

THE CONCEPT of multidisciplinary area study is not as new or as revolutionary as it is sometimes assumed to be. Education in the classics, based on a venerable tradition, also involves multi-faceted study of a whole society. Students of the civilizations of Greece and Rome are not only expected to have a grasp of the language and philology, the literature and mythology of these cultures, but are also required to be well versed in their history, institutions, economies, and social structure. An important difference, it is true, is that classical education is concerned with societies that no longer exist, while area studies as they have developed in the last few decades have examined recent or contemporary societies still in a dynamic process of development and change—often very rapid change.

Although experimental programs in American civilization and in the study of foreign cultures in their entirety date back to the 1920's and 1930's, the Second World War provided the major impetus for the recent remarkable

22

growth of area studies in the United States. Deficiencies in our knowledge of many areas of the world, and the lack of Americans who knew these areas well, were starkly revealed under the pressure of global conflict and of our growing international commitments. After the war government officials, scholars, university administrators, and foundation planners cooperated in efforts to remedy this situation, and several graduate area study programs were initiated. Because of the importance of the Soviet Union and its emerging role in world affairs, programs on the Russian area were among the first to be established in the postwar period. These programs have now been in existence for a little over a decade and have made an excellent record of achievement.

The purpose of this chapter is to review this record and to raise and discuss, on the basis of the experience accumulated, a number of the most important issues connected with graduate study of Russia. Both multidisciplinary area training as it is practiced in the graduate area programs and the more traditional form of graduate education in Russian studies—specialization on Russia in a single discipline—are considered. Area training, in the technical sense, has been one of the most significant developments in Russian studies. Russian area programs have trained the bulk of the new generation of scholars in this field, and they have developed many fruitful ideas of substance and method. At the same time, customary graduate-school methods have throughout the past decade continued to carry a share of graduate education in Russian studies.

The present report is based on visits to seventeen uni-

23

versities having graduate programs in Russian studies[1] and on detailed questionnaires sent to most of these universities and to over six hundred students and alumni of the four largest graduate programs—at the universities of California (Berkeley), Columbia, Harvard, and Washington. Two hundred and eighteen students and alumni, over one-third, replied to the questionnaires. In addition, a number of leading scholars in the field, as well as government officials concerned with education in Russian studies, were consulted.[2]

To a considerable degree the discussion in this chapter takes its departure from the objectives for Russian area study set forth in 1947 by the Committee on World Area Research of the Social Science Research Council, although those suggestions pertained primarily to multidisciplinary area training while this report, as already noted, also considers graduate specialization on Russia in a single discipline. The objectives established in 1947 for area training in the Russian field were: to prepare a limited number of

1. The following universities were visited: California (Berkeley), California (Los Angeles), Chicago, Columbia, Fordham, Harvard, Indiana, Michigan, Michigan State, Minnesota, Notre Dame, Stanford, Syracuse, Texas, Washington, Wayne, and Yale.

2. Drafts of this chapter were discussed at conferences of scholars and administrators in the Russian field on December 6-7, 1957, in New York, and on March 29-30, 1958, in Berkeley, California. The chapter attempts to take account of the views expressed during these conferences and other consultations.

The authors are indebted to the deans and other university administrators, to those supervising and teaching Russian studies, and to the government officials who cooperated in the collection of material for this report. They gave generously of their time and experience, providing ideas and opinions as well as detailed information.

superior students for teaching and research and for non-academic work on the Russian area; to provide competence in the language, on the area, and in a discipline (requiring an additional year of graduate study); and to make students aware of the contribution of disciplines other than their major ones to an understanding of the area. Related goals were the development of disciplines under-represented in Russian studies and of competence on non-Russian areas of the Soviet Union, the preparation of teaching materials and aids, and the provision of research opportunities.[3]

A number of the issues raised in 1947 are now being carefully reconsidered by administrators and scholars concerned with Russian studies. Several of the graduate programs are in the process of re-evaluating their efforts. Since 1947 a good deal of experience in Russian area programs at the graduate level and in the more traditional forms of graduate education in Russian studies has been accumulated, and resources for teaching and research on Russia have been greatly expanded. Opportunities for contact with the Soviet Union have developed rapidly in the last few years. Academic and public interest in the Russian area has burgeoned, and the passage in 1958 of the National Defense Education Act may make available substantial new sources of support and encouragement for the development of area and language study of Russia, as well as of other areas. The time seems appropriate for some

3. Robert B. Hall, *Area Studies*, SSRC Pamphlet No. 3 (New York, 1947), pp. 40-41; and Charles Wagley, *Area Research and Training*, SSRC Pamphlet No. 6 (New York, 1948), pp. 41-43.

reflection concerning the problems and opportunities of graduate education in Russian studies.

II

Evolving Objectives. The primary stimulus to Russian studies in the period immediately following World War II was the desire to understand the new world power which was emerging as the leading rival of the United States in international relations. Russian studies also shared the objectives of foreign area studies in general: to broaden the horizons of American education through study of significant portions of the total human experience that had been largely ignored in the past; to provide perspective and deeper insights into Western culture through an examination of other cultures; and to develop new techniques for the integrated study of a whole society, leading to the breaking down of the restrictive compartmentalization of disciplines and eventually to greater universality of knowledge. At the same time, the chief tasks confronting Russian studies immediately after the war were immediate and practical ones: to provide verified knowledge concerning the Soviet Union and to prepare Americans in this field for careers in government, journalism, and academic life.

Many of the leaders of the movement to develop Russian area studies had served with the government during the war in policy and research capacities, and they knew well how few civil servants were equipped with a working knowledge of the Russian language or an understanding of the Soviet system. The resources for teaching and scholarship on the Russian area were also scanty, although the skills of the handful of scholars trained before and during the war were now supplemented by the experience gained from wartime experiments in Russian area training. In the 1930's, Soviet Russia was on the far horizons of American political and intellectual interests, and during the war Germany and Japan received first priority as areas deserving of systematic study. When in 1945 the Soviet state came to occupy the center of the stage, the United States government as well as the academic community was in most respects unprepared.

Thanks to the farsighted planning and dedication of a few scholars, university administrators, and foundation officials, this challenge was successfully met. Several graduate Russian area programs were established early in the postwar years, hundreds of students who later entered academic life and government service were trained, and our store of knowledge concerning the Soviet Union was rapidly expanded.

Today there exists in the country a new sense of national need, a heightened atmosphere of urgency, concerning our knowledge and understanding of the Soviet orbit. For the first time there is widespread and popular feeling that most educated Americans should know something about the Soviet system and Communism generally. A decade ago there was also a sense of urgency, but it then related to the pressing need for specialized personnel and information concerning Soviet society. Now the interest in Russia is greater, the concern both broader and more complex. This alteration in public and political attitudes,

27

partially reflected in the National Defense Education Act, coincides with the beginning of a major expansion of American higher education, necessitated by the combined effect of a rapidly growing population and a sharp increase in the percentage of secondary-school graduates entering college. Taken together, these factors confront Russian studies with great opportunities and major responsibilities for maintaining and improving specialized education and research on Russia and for widening the study of Russia in American education as a whole.

In the light of these considerations, it is becoming increasingly apparent that in many respects more than Russia itself is involved in what has traditionally been known as Russian studies. The Russian language, although it is not native to many of the peoples of the U.S.S.R., is rapidly becoming a world language. In many fields of science, it already rivals German and French in importance. One can imagine the time in the foreseeable future when Russian will be second only to English as the language of science. In the nineteenth century Russia produced one of the great world literatures which continues to influence intellectual and artistic developments in many other parts of the world as well as in Russia. In the case of economics, the Soviet economy is the prototype of the planned economy and as such is characteristic of the systems under which approximately a third of the world's population now lives. It deserves study as the principal rival to the free pluralistic systems in the underdeveloped countries. Similarly, the Soviet political system, whether considered as a totalitarian

28

government or as an expression of Communist theory, is of significance far beyond the frontiers of the U.S.S.R. In the behavioral sciences, the Soviet Union provides an example of an industrialized, bureaucratic society, while other Communist nations reflect societies in various stages of transition and modernization. From the historical and cultural point of view, the development of Russian civilization represents an important part of the universal human heritage.

This view of Russian studies, significantly broader than that contemplated a decade ago, raises the question of their place in the education of the average American. For many reasons the Russian area is clearly less important than the West European as a subject of general education. In the foreseeable future Western Europe will continue to occupy first place among the foreign areas with which American students should become familiar. It is questionable, however, whether Western Europe should continue to dominate the educational scene so completely. Since World War II we have become aware that we live in a world much larger than the North Atlantic community. The rest of the world was never as quiescent as one would gather from reading course offerings of two decades ago; but it is now so active that even the high walls which protect university curricula have been decisively pierced. The educated citizen must now learn about a new world, and in this new world Russia plays an important role. Its language, literature, and national history give Russia a position of considerable significance. Its political, economic,

29

and social way of life, however, makes it second in importance only to the North Atlantic system as a subject for American study and research.

It may therefore be said that Russian studies have been developing over the past few years from a relatively esoteric subject, of critical interest primarily to government officials and a few scholars, to a subject of general interest and importance for educated citizens who wish to understand the world in which they live. Those concerned with Russian studies are facing the challenge of transferring their high level of specialized achievement to general education. The implications of this challenge for graduate education in Russian studies are considerable. If more colleges and secondary schools in the United States are to meet the need for a wider knowledge of the Russian language and a clearer comprehension of the type of economy, political system, and society of which the Soviet Union is today the leading representative, the graduate schools, in turn, must provide the teachers, researchers, and materials to support such a development. In fact, it is perhaps not far-fetched to foresee the day when every university, almost every college, and many secondary schools will teach the Russian language and will have instructors in at least several fields who are well acquainted with the Russian area and its problems.

As the other papers in this volume show, there are great potentialities for the development of Russian studies in undergraduate and secondary education. Many students and teachers are anxious to know more about the Soviet Union and the Communist system. Many administrators

30

would welcome an opportunity to introduce more material on Russia into the curriculum; they need only advice and guidance on how to begin, and help in finding instructors prepared to teach about Russia and in acquiring the necessary library resources. Graduate education in Russian studies must be ready to encourage and assist this developing interest and to support the widening study of Russia at all levels in American education.

While the opportunities beckoning in the field of Russian studies in undergraduate and secondary education are of great importance, the original objectives of graduate education in Russian studies must not be lost sight of. The demands of national interest which inspired the growth of Russian studies a decade ago continue to play a vital role in their development. The need for well-trained government officials with Russian area competence continues at a rate only a little below that of the first decade. The universities and the scholarly world as a whole still require highly skilled teachers and researchers on the Russian area. Graduate education and research programs will continue to be the core of Russian studies; they remain the indispensable base on which an expansion of Russian studies in undergraduate and secondary education must rest. Their specialized functions must be maintained and reinforced while new approaches in general education are being developed, tested, and applied.

What are the resources available to the Russian field for continuing to fulfill its original assignments as well as for undertaking the new tasks facing it? In appraising the position of Russian studies in the United States today, one is forcibly struck by how much remains to be done as compared with the level of scholarship concerning any of the major West European countries. This is not to say that rapid progress has not been made in the past decade, but rather that the subject is so large and the state of our knowledge ten years ago was so limited that even with the best of efforts only a small part of the task could be completed in so short a time. Moreover, much of the postwar effort in Russian studies centered in a few disciplines: history, literature, economics, and political science. Encouraging beginnings were made in education, geography, linguistics, philosophy, and sociology, but these fields still remain largely unexplored in Russian studies. Almost no scholars were educated or research was undertaken in fine arts, anthropology, archaeology, and the history and sociology of science. The separate papers dealing with American research on Russia since World War II prepared in connection with the Review of Russian Studies illustrate very strikingly the extent of the gap which still exists between Russian and West European studies in regard to the level of our knowledge of each area.[4]

The relatively underdeveloped state of Russian studies is even more apparent in respect to library resources and the availability of teachers. While a number of teachers and scholars have been educated in Russian studies in the last decade, the expected demands resulting from mushrooming enrollments in higher education and from the probable expansion of Russian studies at the undergraduate level are likely to outstrip the supply of Russian specialist

4. See n. 2 of the Introduction.

teachers before long. As a result of the upsurge of interest in Russian language instruction which followed the launching of the Soviet satellites, there is already a critical shortage of teachers of the Russian language for our colleges and high schools, and immediate emergency measures are needed if this shortage is to be overcome. In other disciplines, many of those now teaching courses on Russia have been drafted from other fields of interest and lack specialized preparation on the area.

The shortage of library facilities is also striking. Probably no more than six or seven university libraries have adequate resources for advanced research in Russian studies.[5] Yet research training forms an indispensable part of all types of graduate education in Russian studies.

III

Future Needs. In the light of the evolving objectives of Russian studies, it seems likely that over the next decade there will be continuing need for a wide variety of trained personnel: both nonacademic specialists, including government officials, journalists, and administrators in various international and public information organizations, and scholars in teaching and research, ranging from a small number required by university area centers carrying on advanced graduate education and research to a growing number needed by colleges wishing to offer their undergraduates comparative or special courses dealing with the Russian language, literature, and history, with totalitarian

5. See n. 3 of the Introduction.

33

governments and societies, and with planned economies. While other demands will probably remain at about the present level, a larger number of college teachers equipped to deal with the Russian aspects of their own discipline will undoubtedly be required in a period of growing interest in Russian studies and of an expanding undergraduate population.

On the basis of current resources and a realistic estimate of the support available for the future development of the field, how can we best prepare the various types of personnel needed? There are two basic patterns of graduate education in Russian studies which can be utilized: (1) Full-fledged area programs providing a multidisciplinary introduction to the area at the M. A. level followed by a Ph. D. in a discipline. In its most advanced form, such preparation should also require the student to participate in an interdisciplinary research seminar and to have some acquaintance, for comparative purposes, with another major non-Western area. Complete area training of this type usually requires at least an additional year and a half of study beyond that normally required for a Ph. D. (2) Regular graduate education in Russian studies through specialization on Russia in a single discipline. This should include intensive study of the Russian aspect of that discipline, command of the Russian language, a dissertation topic in the Russian field, and whatever course work is possible in the Russian aspects of other disciplines. (These two patterns are discussed in detail in later sections of the chapter.)

In the years ahead the bulk of the students should be

educated, as they have been during the past decade, in the full-fledged area programs. This is the most complete type of education in Russian studies, providing multidisciplinary area training and encouraging integrated study of the area as a whole. It prepares highly specialized teachers and researchers for the field and, by selective utilization of various levels or components of its total program, it can also provide training for those who wish to acquire a general knowledge of the area without specializing in it. For example, by taking one or two years of the multidisciplinary area program at the M. A. level, those interested in government service, those preparing for nonacademic careers, and college teachers who wish to enrich their teaching by adding familiarity with the Russian area to their disciplinary competence can acquire some background on the area.

At the same time it should be recognized that the area programs will probably not be able to meet the entire range of personnel needs in the field during the next decade. In the first place, the number of full-fledged programs is small. The very extensive resources in staff, courses, and library facilities that are necessary to support full area training are difficult and expensive to acquire and maintain; such resources now exist at only a few institutions and can be developed elsewhere only slowly. Secondly, the future needs of the colleges suggest the desirability of providing opportunities for those students and teachers who wish to acquire a general knowledge of the Russian area, primarily in their discipline, without developing highly specialized competence regarding it. Students may prefer a program of this type because of their intellectual interests or career objectives, or because of limitations of time and money affecting their graduate education.

It seems likely, therefore, that in the coming decade, in addition to the students educated in the full-fledged area programs, a significant number of students will be prepared by traditional graduate-school methods through specialization on Russia in a single discipline. Moreover, special programs, ranging from six to fifteen months' duration, should be considered for established college teachers who wish to broaden their interests by adding general training in the Russian area to their previously acquired disciplinary competence. Such programs should be under the supervision of the area centers. At the same time summer institutes or workshops and consulting services would be of value to secondary-school teachers and others interested in a briefer introduction to the area. Both the area programs and the graduate schools with less developed resources in Russian studies should undertake to direct projects of this kind, in cooperation with schools of education and educational associations. These various programs of teacher education may require some extra-university financing, greater flexibility in training requirements, and a modest expansion or reallocation of administrative and faculty resources in Russian studies in institutions meeting these new needs. The provisions of the National Defense Education Act may be of some assistance in establishing and maintaining special training projects of this kind, particularly where language study is involved.

In general, it may be said that the coming years will

36

require a continuation and development of graduate education in Russian studies in all the directions indicated above if the field is to capitalize on its opportunities and fulfill its responsibilities to the educational community and to the nation at large. Present area programs should be strengthened and improved, particularly in the light of the experience of the past decade. The programs should make a special effort to take advantage of the growing opportunities for contact with the Soviet Union and of the improved grounding in the Russian language and area that students entering the programs in the future can be expected to have as a result of the increasing interest in Russian studies at the undergraduate and secondary-school levels. One or two additional programs properly equipped to provide full area training should be developed as resources permit. In view of the present concentration of area programs on the East and West coasts, these programs may well, and suitably, emerge in the Midwest. The development of one or two well-staffed and adequately supported programs, prepared to do the complex and demanding job inherent in complete area training, would be far more desirable than the establishment of a number of "paper" programs, commanding insufficient resources and ostensibly offering training they are not equipped to give. While the assistance provided by the National Defense Education Act may be of considerable value in strengthening existing area programs and in developing new ones, the availability of experienced scholars and teachers and of library materials in Russian studies is limited. Care must

37

be taken that the Act does not encourage spreading the scarce resources of the field too thin or lead to the depletion of present centers of strength in Russian studies.

A number of institutions which now possess certain resources in Russian studies, though not enough to support full area training, can fulfill an important function by providing well-developed graduate specialization on Russia in one or more individual disciplines to students anxious to acquire some knowledge of the area. In this way, they will help to meet the need for college teachers who can include coverage of the Russian area in their general undergraduate teaching. At the same time, by playing a role in the preparation of college teachers and in the "in-service" education of secondary-school teachers through workshops and institutes, these graduate institutions, as well as the area programs, can become significant centers of influence for the promotion of Russian studies in various geographical regions of the country.[6]

IV

General Requirements of Graduate Education on Russia. Certain basic issues affect all patterns of graduate education in Russian studies. A much debated question is the amount of work in the Russian language and area an undergraduate should take in preparation for graduate study of the area. One view, widely supported in the Russian field,

6. For a fuller discussion of the role of the area programs and of the universities with more limited resources in Russian studies in encouraging and assisting the study of Russia in undergraduate and secondary education, see pp. 101-10 of this chapter, and the succeeding chapters.

is that the best undergraduate background for students either entering multidisciplinary graduate area programs or undertaking specialization on Russia in a single discipline is general preparation in the social sciences and humanities, sufficient grounding in a single discipline to permit the beginning of disciplinary work at the graduate level without delay, and adequate language preparation. To the extent possible within this framework, it is probably also desirable for undergraduates to take a few courses that will serve to introduce them to the area. In this view, intensive specialization in the area at the undergraduate level is a mistake. Only a minority of the students taking undergraduate programs on Russia can be expected to go on to graduate work in the Russian field. Even for the student who does so, undergraduate concentration in the area reduces the amount of time available for study of his own culture and heritage and for general preparation in the liberal arts, which should be primary objectives of an undergraduate education. In graduate school the student will be plunged into intensive specialization in a discipline and in the area; he should therefore utilize his college years to acquire the broad educational foundation necessary to support such specialization. The pressure of graduate study will certainly not permit him to add such a foundation at that stage, once he has missed it in his undergraduate experience.

An opposing viewpoint is that undergraduates interested in Russia should be encouraged to major in the area, in addition to undertaking study of the Russian language. It is argued that an area major is as useful for purposes of a

39

general liberal-arts education as the conventional under-graduate majors in a discipline or group of disciplines. In this view, it might even be desirable to require basic area and language work in college for admission to graduate area programs or to graduate study of Russia in a disci-pline. This would reduce the amount of time now devoted in graduate school to elementary language instruction and to survey courses on the area. Such a requirement might also encourage the spread of Russian studies in under-graduate institutions.

In this connection, it should be noted that several of the existing graduate programs in Russian studies grew out of and are largely extensions of undergraduate majors on the Russian area. Some observers see distinct advantages in a close relationship between programs on Russia at the grad-uate and undergraduate levels in the same university. They believe that undergraduate majors in the area stimulate student and university interest in graduate training on Russia, provide experience and resources upon which the graduate programs can draw, and prepare students for graduate training in the field. Others, while recognizing the benefits of arousing undergraduate interest in Russia and of having students who are going on to graduate school begin language training at the undergraduate level, main-tain that too close a relationship between graduate and undergraduate programs in Russian studies within one university may blur the distinction in attainment and pur-pose between graduate and undergraduate education, lower the quality of the graduate training, and orient the undergraduate program toward vocational rather than cultural objectives.

An encouraging and significant development for all forms of graduate education in Russian studies is the increasing percentage of students entering the graduate area programs with one year or more of previous training in the Russian language and with some prior acquaintance with the Russian area—acquired either in college or in military training programs. For example, of twenty-two students not of Russian origin who entered the graduate programs at Columbia and Harvard in 1948 and who replied to the questionnaire sent them by the Subcommittee on Review, only forty-five per cent had already had one year or more of Russian language training and only twenty-seven per cent had previously studied Russia and the Soviet Union. On the other hand, of twenty American students entering in 1955 who replied to the questionnaire, ninety per cent had previously taken Russian for one year or more and seventy per cent had undertaken prior study of the area. If, as expected, more undergraduate colleges develop course work in the Russian language and area in the years ahead, the percentage of students beginning graduate study of Russia with some grounding in the language and some acquaintance with the area should continue to rise. Thus, the next decade may see the virtual elimination of the considerable handicap under which graduate education in Russian studies has labored in the past—that of providing elementary instruction in the language and area to many of the graduate students enter-

41

ing this field.[7] This will permit more intensive concentration in the area and in a discipline for almost all students.

Language Training. Command of the Russian language is indispensable for almost all types of graduate education in Russian studies. Both the student in the multidisciplinary area program and the student concentrating on the Russian aspect of a single discipline should have good facility in reading, speaking, and understanding Russian. For those in literature and related fields, virtually complete mastery of the language is essential. As opportunities to travel and study in the Soviet Union expand, fluency in speaking and understanding Russian takes on increasing importance.

The proposed development of special postgraduate programs for established college teachers who desire to add a general background on the area to previous disciplinary competence, and of summer workshops or institutes for secondary-school teachers and others interested in a briefer introduction to the area, raises the question of whether command of the Russian language, sometimes considered the dividing line between the specialist and the nonspecialist, should be required in these cases. This will probably have to be decided on an individual basis. College teachers undertaking fifteen months of postgraduate training in the Russian area should probably be encouraged to study the Russian language throughout this period. Others, involved

7. The extent of this handicap is indicated by the fact that thirty per cent of the 202 students not of Russian origin who answered the Subcommittee questionnaire had had less than one year of previous Russian language training when they entered the graduate programs; forty per cent had not studied the area previously.

42

in shorter programs, may or may not wish to study Russian, depending on their objectives, interests, and abilities. One difference between the situation now and that which existed in 1946 is that many excellent studies of Russia in English have been published in the last decade. The teacher who lacks a knowledge of Russian is thus less handicapped than he was ten years ago.

The graduate area programs have made considerable progress in language training during the past decade. All of the graduate programs call for proficiency in reading Russian at some stage of the training process. Two programs (Harvard and California) require at least one year of intensive Russian for admission, but exceptions are frequently made for students well qualified in other respects. Most of the other programs prefer to admit students with previous Russian language training, but also recognize that there are many able applicants from undergraduate institutions which do not offer work in the Russian language.

Of the four largest area programs (California, Columbia, Harvard, and Washington), only Harvard requires some proficiency in speaking as well as reading Russian. None demands an ability to write Russian. Proficiency in reading and speaking is sometimes tested through course work, sometimes through special written and oral examinations. In most programs, students are supposed to have acquired sufficient proficiency in reading to do research in Russian by the end of the first year and at least prior to doing seminar work in the field. In practice not many students who enter the programs with little or no Russian are

43

equipped to do rapid research in Russian by their second year. As a result, their seminar papers and master's essays often draw heavily on non-Russian or translated materials.

In addition to Russian, most programs require one West European language. Several advise study of another Slavic or East European language and recommend advanced work in Russian beyond the minimum requirements. Of those students replying to the Subcommittee questionnaire, however, only twelve per cent had studied another Slavic or East European language and only forty per cent had taken any advanced Russian.

The four largest programs all offer Russian language training on a variety of levels, from elementary intensive to advanced conversation and composition. Advanced language training oriented toward the subject or discipline interests of various groups of second-year students in the programs (e.g., vocabulary and materials in economics) is given only occasionally, chiefly because of the expense involved. Almost all programs utilize recently developed techniques of language teaching to some degree—intensive courses, use of informants or tutorials, early oral practice—but the restricted amount of time the student in the area program has available for language training tends to reduce the value of this approach. Language-laboratory facilities are not generally available.

Student opinion on the effectiveness of their Russian language training in the area programs was almost evenly divided. Of respondents, 55 per cent believed that their language training was good or adequate, while 45 per cent felt that it was inadequate. The chief reasons advanced

44

for the inadequacy of language training were insufficient time and practice on the language, too heavy an emphasis in the training on reading skills with a consequent neglect of speaking ability, instruction of poor quality, and the student's own difficulty or lack of application in language study.

Many teachers in the Russian area programs, both those offering the Russian language and those in the social sciences and humanities, also expressed the opinion that language training in the programs should be improved. They pointed out that five major problems made it difficult to provide the kind of language training that would produce students with satisfactory proficiency in Russian: the necessity of providing many beginning graduate students with elementary language instruction; lack of time for really intensive study and practice in the language when students are already carrying a full graduate course load; emphasis on reading skills for research purposes and insufficient opportunities for aural-oral instruction and practice; lack of basic language teaching aids, such as good texts and supplementary materials; and inadequate utilization of modern teaching techniques—tapes, language laboratories, film strips, and other aids—sometimes because of inadequate funds, sometimes because of a pedagogical adherence to traditional methods of instruction.

There are grounds, however, for considerable optimism in regard to language training. Progress is being made in solving all of the problems noted above. As interest in Russian studies spreads in colleges and secondary schools across the country, vigorous efforts should be made to encourage the introduction of basic instruction in the Russian language in as many institutions as possible. The increasingly accepted view that in the future the Russian language will be a generally useful tool not only for area specialists but also for scientists, government officials, and many other Americans can be utilized to support such efforts.

As instruction in the Russian language develops in the colleges and secondary schools, consideration should be given to requiring at least one year's training in Russian as a prerequisite for graduate study of Russia. At the very least, students should be required, upon their acceptance in graduate school, to spend the summer prior to admission in intensive study of the Russian language. Such a requirement will not impose an undue burden on the student in view of the expected availability of special summer language institutes, usually with scholarship funds at hand, whose establishment is encouraged under the provisions of Title VI of the National Defense Education Act. If almost all students embarking on graduate study of Russia have some basic language preparation, language instruction at the graduate level can then be focused on intermediate and advanced work and on the development of full proficiency in Russian.

Other steps are already being taken to improve training in the Russian language. Better texts and materials are being prepared, and there is a growing realization of the importance of utilizing modern technical aids. Several area programs have developed or are developing language laboratories, and others will undoubtedly follow suit.

Most significantly, perhaps, increasing emphasis is being placed on the ability to speak and understand Russian. It is generally agreed that many students educated in the past decade were inadequately prepared in this regard. In the years ahead it would perhaps be desirable to require students to take at least one lecture and discussion course conducted in Russian. In addition, the possibility of traveling and studying in the Soviet Union furnishes an important incentive for the development of aural-oral skills; and such experiences provide the best possible method for practicing and perfecting these skills.

Disciplinary Training. Mastery of the skills of a discipline is another essential component of all patterns of graduate education in Russian studies. Every student should receive training in an academic discipline equivalent to that received by other graduate students who are not specializing in the area. If this is done, all students will have sufficient grasp of a single discipline to be able to use it as a tool of analysis in studying the problems of the Russian area. The objective of area training should be to add another skill—competence in the area—to a basic disciplinary skill, not to substitute area knowledge for disciplinary competence.

At present a number of graduate area programs do not make adequate provision for disciplinary training. Although they generally require concentration in one or more disciplines in the Russian field (e.g., in Russian and Soviet government) and recommend course work in the student's major discipline outside the Russian field (e.g., in American government, comparative government, public administra-

47

tion), they grant the M. A. degree in Russian area studies, and the student seldom receives training in a discipline equivalent to that received by graduate students not in the area program. Only the program at Columbia demands the fulfillment of requirements for two degrees—an M. A. in a discipline and an area certificate. At Columbia the area student must meet exactly the same requirements for the discipline degree as any graduate student in the discipline department. It should be noted, however, that in general the definition and measurement of training in a discipline is difficult, since degree standards, particularly for the M. A., vary widely from university to university and even among departments within one university.

Those who support the idea of granting an M. A. in Russian area studies without equivalent concentration in a discipline maintain that disciplinary training is not essential at the M. A. level. It is argued that the majority of students at that level are being prepared for government service, where specialized competence in a discipline is considered less valuable than a general knowledge of the area. In this view, students who go on for the Ph. D. receive enough disciplinary work in the course of their area M. A. to ground them adequately in a discipline and to permit them rapidly to meet the departmental requirements for the Ph. D. in a discipline.

Many of the graduates of the area programs believe, however, that the amount of training in a discipline they received while acquiring an area M. A. was insufficient to prepare them for further academic work. In a few cases students with an area M. A. who wished to continue toward

48

a Ph. D. in a discipline reportedly found it necessary virtually to begin graduate study in the discipline all over again. They had to go back and take much of the fundamental work in the discipline required of first-year graduate students in the discipline department. Even Columbia's double requirement, both an M. A. in a discipline and an area certificate, did not provide entirely satisfactory disciplinary training, in the opinion of some graduates of that program. They claim that their twofold training was so intensive and heavy that their disciplinary work suffered. While they had to, and could just barely, meet the minimum requirements in the discipline, other graduate students in the discipline had an opportunity to master the discipline more thoroughly, taking a wider variety of courses and doing more reading and seminar work. Some graduates of Columbia who went into teaching feel that their disciplinary training was weighted heavily toward one substantive specialty (e.g., political institutions) and its application to the Russian area; as a result, they were not equipped to teach the broad general courses or the variety of courses in the discipline that are normally required of the beginning college instructor.

Almost all observers agree, however, that advanced graduate work in the Russian field should be in a discipline. The student interested in the Russian area should fulfill the same requirements for the Ph. D. in a discipline as other graduate students in the discipline department. The Ph. D. degree should be in the discipline, not in Russian area studies. Under such a program, the student emerges from his graduate preparation with a double competence—

49

fundamental training in a discipline combined with thorough knowledge of the Russian area—and is better equipped for both research and teaching. In research he has acquired the analytical tools necessary to scholarly investigation, as well as a broad understanding of the Russian setting in which his problem is placed. In teaching he is prepared not only to offer courses dealing with the Russian aspect of his discipline but also to share in the teaching of general courses in the discipline; he is therefore more easily placed in college and university departments.

V

Graduate Education in Russian Area Programs. The area approach to graduate education and research has received its chief stimulus and application since World War II. The supporters of the area approach, including those in Russian studies, believe that it can make an important and unique contribution to the general goal of all scholarly endeavor in the social sciences and humanities—the advancement of knowledge concerning man's institutions, values, and behavior. In the first place, area study is an attempt to understand a whole society by applying, and relating to each other, a variety of disciplinary analyses of that society. In the area approach, an effort is made to advance beyond single or even multidisciplinary study of a society to an integrated, interdisciplinary comprehension of its totality. In this process, it is believed, the increasing specialization and isolation of the individual disciplines in American academic life can be broken down and the essential functional unity of all knowledge can be demonstrated. From this effort, new scholarly attitudes, new insights, and new techniques can be expected to emerge.

Secondly, the area approach represents an attempt to provide information and comparative data on a number of societies, including many in the non-Western world. Much of the theoretical development of the social science and humane disciplines has been based solely on material provided by or applicable to the North Atlantic community alone. Area study, where it is concerned with non-Western areas, can help to overcome this provincialism of American scholarship and can assist in the development of generalizations possessing greater universality.

Finally, the area approach can lead to the development of new perspectives and a deeper understanding of Western society itself. Through a recognition of cultural differences and an appreciation of diverse institutional patterns, we learn to know ourselves better.

In the case of Russia, the area approach is especially important and pertinent. As a result of its past neglect in conventional discipline study, our level of knowledge concerning this significant area is alarmingly low. Extraordinary efforts are required to overcome this deficiency. In addition, because of the uniqueness of many Russian and Soviet institutions and because of the integrated nature of Soviet society, this area is peculiarly suited to the application of the area approach.

At the same time there are some who contend that the area approach is essential for the study of a society only under certain special conditions: for example, when the

51

area is inaccessible or when little is known about it. As we learn more about Russia, as the store of knowledge and the analytical techniques of the various disciplines as applied to the Russian area are increased and strengthened, and as access to the area improves, the need for the area approach in studying Russia will decrease, it is argued. Thus, at some future time, area study of Russia may "wither away."

Achievements of the Postwar Decade. The growth of area studies, and particularly Russian studies, following World War II constitutes an important chapter in the annals of American graduate education. Prior to the war there were only a few scholars specializing in the Russian field. A few more completed their education during the war, and a number of students were introduced to the area through the Army Specialized Training Program and other wartime educational experiments. In 1946 little scholarly and research material on Russia was available. Only a few studies of Tsarist and Soviet society had been published, and those were predominantly in history and literature, the disciplines customarily associated with the study of Russia in American academic life. The area programs established at the end of the war had few resources in teaching and scholarship, and almost no tradition, on which to build. Centers of Russian studies had not existed before the war, and the concept of integrated study of a foreign area was largely untested.

Today, little more than a decade later, Russian studies have been transformed into a vigorous and flourishing field with an outstanding record of achievement in graduate education and research. Since 1946 two large and productive centers of Russian studies, at Columbia and at Harvard, have been established. Additional area centers have been set up at California and at Washington, and several universities have developed smaller graduate programs on the Russian area. In addition, a number of other graduate schools have provided some preparation in Russian studies through course offerings or specialization on Russia in one or more individual disciplines, and several colleges have launched undergraduate programs on the Russian area.

Between 1946 and 1956 over five hundred students completed one- or two-year M. A.'s in the Russian field. Of these, Columbia alone educated approximately 235 students who acquired double graduate degrees, an M. A. in a discipline and a certificate on the area. Almost 200 students received a single degree, an M. A. in Russian area studies; the Harvard program prepared approximately 100 of these, while the remainder were scattered among the other graduate Russian area programs throughout the country. An indeterminate but probably smaller number of students received an M. A. in a discipline with specialization in the Russian aspect of that discipline. Most of the students who acquired an M. A. in the Russian field either continued graduate study toward the Ph. D. or entered government service; a small percentage embarked on careers in journalism, radio, and private organizations interested in Russian or foreign affairs.

In the same period approximately 50 Ph. D.'s were granted to students who both specialized on Russia in a single discipline and completed a multidisciplinary area program during their training (primarily at Columbia and Harvard). Roughly 30 Ph. D.'s were granted to students who specialized on Russia in a single discipline but did not complete an area program. Another 70 or 80 individuals who began graduate study of Russia during the last ten years are still pursuing advanced work toward a Ph. D. Between 1946 and 1956 the graduate Russian area programs also educated a considerable number of government personnel, about two dozen foreign students and scholars, and a few postdoctoral scholars.

At the same time, sometimes as an integral part of the training process, sometimes separately, the graduate area programs produced a substantial body of research on Russia. Additional research in Russian studies was carried on under government contract or auspices.

In short, the past decade has witnessed a virtual revolution in Russian studies. New techniques in education have been developed and applied with considerable success. A sizable new generation of scholars, teachers, and government officials has been educated and is entering upon productive careers. A promising beginning has been made in understanding Russian and Soviet society, and much basic research on Russia has been accomplished, despite the inaccessibility of the area. Interest in Russian studies on the part of universities and colleges has grown and is still increasing.

This progress was made possible largely through the careful planning and effective cooperation of the universities and the foundations and through the devotion and skilled leadership of the senior scholars in Russian studies who initiated this development and worked unsparingly to bring it to fruition. This was a pioneering effort, requiring imagination, dedication, and much hard work. The result is a remarkable achievement, of which the institutions and men responsible and the nation as a whole may be justly proud.

Generous foundation support permitted the establishment and strengthening of several specialized centers for graduate education and research in Russian studies. In addition, the foundations financed research and publication projects, the improvement of library resources, and national fellowship programs, which helped the field to attract some of the very best of the postwar graduate students. The total foundation contribution to Russian studies amounted to several million dollars. At the same time the universities, both those which developed their programs with the help of foundation grants and those which did so entirely with their own resources, invested heavily in Russian studies. Universities bore most of the costs of instruction and also contributed substantially to library resources and fellowships and to overhead and administration expenses. The total university investment in Russian studies substantially surpassed even the sizable amount provided by the foundations. But the development of Russian studies was largely a joint enterprise and neither partner in it could have succeeded without the guidance and assistance of the other.

Of the dozen or so special graduate programs in Russian studies now in existence,[8] roughly half were established

8. There are special graduate programs in Russian studies at:
University of California: Center of Slavic and East European Studies

during or immediately after the war. The remainder were founded in the 1950's. The size and intensity of these programs differ considerably. The Russian Institute of Columbia University admits approximately forty new students every year and has enrolled over four hundred and fifty since the war. Harvard's Regional Program on the Soviet Union annually admits about twenty students, and has had a total postwar enrollment of roughly one hundred and fifty. On the other hand, some programs admit only a half a dozen or fewer new students each year and have educated less than twenty individuals during the postwar period. The great majority of students have been educated in programs on the East Coast, some in programs on the West Coast, and a small number in programs in the Midwest. Other sections of the country do not have graduate Russian area programs. A few of the programs require concentrated, intensive study over two years with a work load considerably greater than that carried by the graduate student not in an area program. Others call for

---

Columbia University: The Russian Institute
Fordham University: Institute of Contemporary Russian Studies
Harvard University: Regional Program on the Soviet Union
Indiana University: Russian and East European Institute
University of Michigan: Degree Program in Russian Studies
University of Minnesota: Center for International Relations and Area Studies, Subcommittee on Russia
University of Notre Dame: Studies in Soviet Policy and Eastern Europe
Syracuse University: Board of Russian Studies
University of Washington: Far Eastern and Russian Institute
Wayne State University: Committee on East European Studies
University of Wisconsin: Russian Area Studies Program
Yale University: Program of Graduate Studies—Russia

little more study than that required in a normal one-year M. A. program.

The programs also vary widely in their geographic and language coverage. Roughly half treat only the area of the Soviet Union and offer Russian language training primarily. The program at the University of Washington is linked closely with a Far Eastern studies program. The rest include the Russian area in general Slavic or East European studies programs, sometimes as a separate major or concentration, sometimes indistinguishably fused with study of the whole East European area. From one to several Slavic or East European languages are offered in addition to the Russian language. Few of the programs devote much attention to any of the national minority areas of the Soviet Union; if dealt with at all, this field is covered through a general survey of the nationalities or in a course on Russian colonization. Only occasionally are Ukrainian or other non-Russian languages of the U.S.S.R. taught.

Two-thirds of the programs recognize the completion of study by granting an M. A. degree in Russian area studies. Only Columbia's Russian Institute, and the newly established programs at Indiana and Wisconsin, require that students earn a double degree, an M. A. in a discipline and a certificate in area studies. Several programs grant either an M. A. in Russian area studies or an M. A. in a discipline with Russian specialization. They do not require students to obtain both degrees, although a few individuals have done so.

Half of the programs make no provision at all for Ph. D. work. The University of California at Berkeley has offered a Ph. D. in Slavic studies in the past but no longer does so.

TABLE I-1. INSTITUTIONS OF ORIGIN FOR STUDENTS ENTERING RUSSIAN
PROGRAMS AT COLUMBIA AND HARVARD, 1946-1956

Institution of Origin	At Columbia	At Harvard	Total
Columbia	39	1	40
Harvard	19	17	36
C.C.N.Y.	17	4	21
Cornell	16	3	19
Michigan	11	7	18
Princeton	9	7	16
Dartmouth	10	4	14
Wisconsin	10	3	13
Brown	9	2	11
Northwestern	11	0	11
Syracuse	7	4	11
Chicago	8	2	10
California	8	1	9
Washington	9	0	9
Yale	9	0	9
Bryn Mawr	6	2	8
Rutgers	4	4	8
Swarthmore	7	1	8
Smith	4	4	8
N.Y.U.	7	0	7
Brooklyn	5	1	6
Colgate	3	3	6
Indiana	4	2	6
Ohio State	5	1	6
Penn State	6	0	6
Stanford	5	1	6
Wesleyan	4	2	6
Bowdoin	4	1	5
Colorado	4	1	5
Fordham	2	3	5
Haverford	3	2	5
Minnesota	4	1	5
Oberlin	4	1	5
Pennsylvania	4	1	5
Vassar	3	2	5
Total	114	34	148

Notes: see next page.

58

Five or six programs guide and assist study toward a Ph. D. in a traditional discipline, with specialization and the doctoral dissertation on the Russian area. The candidate's doctoral sponsor is usually a member of both the discipline department and the area program, but the degree is granted by the discipline department concerned, not by the program. In most cases, prior completion of the area program is recommended for Ph. D. candidates in the Russian field. In some departments at Columbia this recommendation is so strong as to be virtually a requirement, and a majority of Columbia Ph. D.'s specializing on Russia in a single discipline complete the area program in the course of their training. Elsewhere the picture is mixed: some Ph. D.'s with a Russian specialization complete the area program; some do not.

Universities and colleges with undergraduate programs in Russian studies, a tradition of interest in the area, or vigorous Russian specialist teachers provided the bulk of

Notes to Table 1-1:

1. The above figures cover 62 per cent of all students in Russian programs at Columbia and Harvard. The remaining 38 per cent (169 students at Columbia, 57 at Harvard) came from 143 U. S. and foreign institutions. The total number of students whose institutions of origin were known was 594 (Columbia 449, Harvard 145).
2. The majority of the students entering California, Fordham, Indiana, and Notre Dame, the other programs for which figures are available, came from the "host" institutions. Since entrants from other schools were a negligible factor, figures from these programs are not included above.
3. Columbia and Harvard probably did not supply as many undergraduates to their own programs as the above figures might suggest, since graduate transfers to the Russian program from other parts of the university are included.

the students entering graduate Russian area programs in the postwar decade (excluding the "host" institutions of the programs, which in each case were the chief suppliers to their own programs: see Table I-1). The great majority of students beginning graduate Russian area study came from institutions in the Northeast. A surprisingly small number, however, were graduates of the small Eastern liberal arts men's colleges, usually considered major sources of graduate and professional school students. Extremely few entering students were from universities and colleges in the South or Southwest.

Several universities, such as Michigan, Syracuse, and California, which have their own graduate programs on the area also supplied a sizable number of students to the programs at Columbia and Harvard; in each case the university has an active undergraduate program on Russia. Twelve institutions provided 37 per cent of the students admitted by Columbia and Harvard, twenty-three others another 25 per cent, and 143 American and foreign schools the remaining 38 per cent.

A total of 698 students entered the graduate programs at California, Columbia, Harvard, Indiana, and Notre Dame between 1946 and 1956 (Table I-2). Seventy-seven per cent entered as first-year graduate students or with one year or less of graduate training. Those coming into the programs with additional graduate training, graduate or professional degrees (primarily M. A.'s but a few Ph. D.'s and six LL. B.'s), or in some special status comprised 23 per cent of the total. There were 48 foreign students, making up 7 per cent of all the entrants.

TABLE I-2. STUDENTS ENTERING AND COMPLETING GRADUATE M. A. PROGRAMS
IN THE RUSSIAN AREA, 1946-1956

	California	Columbia	Harvard	Indiana	Notre Dame	Totals
Total entrants	17	485	146	30	20	698
Foreign entrants (7% of total)	0	39	3	4	2	48
Undergraduate and early graduate entrants (77% of total)	17	340	138	24	20	539
Advanced graduate or special status entrants (23% of total)	0	145	8	6	0	159
Total completions	14	268	91	24	16	413
Per cent of total entrants completing program	*82*	*55*[a]	*63*	*80*	*80*	*59*
Foreign completions	0	18	1	2	2	23
Per cent of foreign entrants completing program	*0*	*46*	*33.3*	*50*	*100*	*50*
Completions requiring more than normal duration of program	4	50	4	9	0	67
Per cent of total completions requiring extra time	*28*	*18*	*4.5*	*37.5*	*0*	*18*

[a] Early postwar entrants at Columbia had a markedly higher percentage of completion than later classes: e.g., for 1947-48 entrants, 70 per cent; for 1951-52 entrants, 51 per cent.

Note: Statistics were not available for the program at the University of Washington.

61

Of those entering the programs, 413 (59 per cent) completed them (Table I-2). Among foreign students the percentage of completion was 50 per cent. Of those completing the programs, 17 per cent could not do so in the time normally required and needed an additional semester or year to finish their work.

During the postwar decade by far the largest number of students receiving an M. A. in the Russian field either majored or were granted degrees in the related fields of political science, law, and international relations: 183, or 45 per cent of the total M. A.'s (Table I-3). This is understandable if one makes the plausible assumption that the majority of students in Russian area programs who were planning to enter government service selected international relations or government as their disciplinary fields. As might be expected, this dominance by political science-international relations did not carry over to the Ph. D. level, where these fields accounted for only 23 per cent of the total Ph. D.'s. While there are more Ph. D.'s in progress in political science and international relations, undoubtedly a number of these individuals are in government service and will not complete their degrees. History represented 28 per cent of the total number of Ph. D.'s, and language and literature, 24 per cent. Economics was not far behind, with 17 per cent of the Ph. D.'s specializing in that discipline.

The figures in Table I-3 illustrate graphically the underrepresented position in Russian studies of such disciplines as sociology, psychology, anthropology, geography, phi-

TABLE I-3. DEGREES IN RUSSIAN STUDIES BY DISCIPLINES, 1946-1956

	M. A.[a]					Ph. D.					
	Calif.	Col.	Harv.	Total	Per Cent of All M. A.'s	Calif.	Col.	Harv.	Wash.	Total	Per Cent of All Ph. D.'s
History	14	49	35	98	24	8	8	7	0	23	28
Language and literature	9	52	5	66	16	6	10	3	1	20	24
Economics	1	34	14	49	12	1	7	5	1	14	17
International relations	0	86	3	89	22	0	10	0	0	10	12
Political science and law	4	56	34	94	23	1	2	4	2	9	11
Social relations[b]	0	0	8	8	2	0	1	4	0	5	6
Geography	...	...	...	...	...	...	...	...	1	1	1
	28	277	99	404		16	38	23	5	82	

[a] Major discipline where M. A. was in Russian area studies.
[b] Includes sociology, social psychology, and cultural anthropology.

63

losophy, and fine arts: only a handful of people trained, and no indication that many more are in process.

Placement. During the last decade the great majority of students from the Russian area programs, including non-graduates, recipients of the M. A., and those who went on to obtain the Ph. D., found their first positions in teaching, research (academic and government), and operational government careers related to Russian studies and Soviet affairs: 20 per cent, 25 per cent, and 27 per cent respectively (Table I-4). Total academic placement (teaching and full-time research) and total government placement (research and operations) were almost evenly divided—33 per cent and 39 per cent, respectively—and together accounted for almost three-quarters of the students whose first positions are known. Ten per cent of the students entered careers in journalism, radio, business, law, and administration related to Russian studies. Almost one-fifth accepted positions in a wide variety of occupations not connected with Russian studies or Soviet affairs, although well over half of this group were nongraduates of the programs.

Most of those concerned with administering and teaching Russian studies believe that current placement and future employment prospects are good. No major difficulties in placement were reported by the area programs, although a small number of graduates of the programs, primarily those in academic life, indicated that they had not been able to find jobs which they considered desirable in terms of salary and opportunities to develop their specialized area and research interests. Government demand has slacked off a little from its immediate postwar high, while teaching

TABLE I-4. PLACEMENT OF RUSSIAN AREA STUDENTS, 1946-1956
(from Columbia, Harvard, Indiana, and Washington)

Total number of graduates and nongraduates   670 (approx.)
Number continuing graduate training   75
Number whose first position is known   420

	Number	Per Cent of Those Placed
In Russian field		
Teaching	84	20
Academic or private research	53	13
Total academic	137	33
Government research	50	12
Other government (including UN)	112	27
Total government	162	39
Administration	8	2
Business and law	7	1.5
Journalism and radio	28	7
Not in Russian field	78[a]	18.5

[a] Almost one-third in business, some in high-school teaching and military service, and the rest in a wide variety of jobs ranging from actor to factory worker. Over one-half in this category are nongraduates as compared to one-third or one-fourth in other groups.

opportunities seem to be increasing, according to most observers. During 1958 and 1959 there has been a brisk demand for teachers of the Russian language, which can be expected to continue to rise in the years ahead. A shortage of such teachers, if not already existing, is in prospect in the near future.

Government officials estimate that the government will

65

continue to need a slightly reduced but still substantial number of Russian area specialists for the foreseeable future, and that in the long run government demand for such persons will probably grow slowly and steadily. The view that Russian area training provides a useful background for a wide variety of positions in Washington and in the field that are not directly connected with the Soviet area is gaining increasing currency among a number of administrators and operational officials in the government.

Scholarships and Fellowships. Financial assistance to students in graduate Russian area programs was provided in four major ways during the period under review. One of the most important sources of student support was the G. I. Bill, which helped a number of students undertake graduate study of Russia after World War II and after the Korean War, but which is now available to only a few veterans. In addition, scholarships and fellowships of three types were instrumental in encouraging and assisting Russian area students: those provided from university funds, either through regular graduate awards or in special allotments to the Russian programs; those financed through foundation grants to individual Russian area programs; and those made available through national fellowship programs supported by the foundations.

During the postwar decade the largest amount of fellowship support for Russian area students stemmed from national fellowship programs: 165 awards, the majority for both maintenance and tuition. Important sources of assistance in the first half of the decade, between 1946 and 1952, were the general Advanced Graduate and First-Year

Graduate Fellowship Programs in the humanities sponsored by the American Council of Learned Societies (ACLS) under grants from the Rockefeller Foundation. While not specifically for area studies, fellowships under these programs provided support to twenty-one students specializing on Russia in history, literature, and linguistics (Table I-5). In addition, a score or more students who entered Russian studies after the war began their study of the Russian language under the wartime Intensive Language Program of the ACLS.

Two fellowship programs specifically designed to assist students to develop competence in various foreign areas also provided major support for young specialists on Russia during the postwar years. Between 1948 and 1953 the program of Area Research Training Fellowships supervised by the Social Science Research Council under a grant from the Carnegie Corporation made thirty-one awards for late pre-doctoral study, primarily in the social sciences, to students in Russian studies. Between 1954 and 1957 the Foreign Area Training Fellowship Program of the Ford Foundation assisted 113 students and scholars in the Russian field. These fellowships were for both first- or second-year graduate study and later pre-doctoral study. Extensions to support a second or third year of fellowship study were granted in 1956 and 1957 to over forty of these Ford Fellows.

There is little doubt that without the fellowships made available through these national programs and through foundation grants to individual Russian area programs, only a limited number of postwar graduate students would have

67

been able to assume the added burden of time and expense
involved in Russian area study. Moreover, the Russian field

TABLE I-5. NATIONAL FELLOWSHIP AWARDS FOR TRAINING
IN RUSSIAN STUDIES, 1946-1957

Discipline	ACLS[a]	SSRC[b]	Ford[c]	Total	Per Cent of Total Awards
History	6	11	34	51	31
Literature & language	12	2	20	34	21
Political science	...	7	20	27	16
International relations and law	1	4	17	22	13
Economics	...	5	6	11	7
Geography	...	1	6	7	4
Linguistics	2	...	3	5	3
Sociology	...	...	3	3	2
Philosophy	...	...	2	2	1
Area studies	...	1	1	2	1
Anthropology	...	...	1	1	0.5
Total	21	31	113	165	100.0

[a] These awards were not specifically for Russian area studies, but were
made to students in the Russian field between 1946 and 1952 under the
Advanced Graduate and First-Year Graduate Fellowship Programs in the
humanities sponsored by the American Council of Learned Societies and
financed by the Rockefeller Foundation. Some of these awards were
renewed for a second or third year.

[b] These awards were made for late pre-doctoral study, primarily in
the social sciences, under the Area Research Training Fellowship Program of the Social Science Research Council. This program lasted from
1948 to 1953 and was supported by grants from the Carnegie Corporation.

[c] These awards were made between 1954 and 1957 under the Foreign
Area Training Fellowship Program of the Ford Foundation. Awards
were for both first- or second-year graduate study and later pre-doctoral
study. In 1956 and 1957, over forty of these awards were extended to
support a second or third year of fellowship study.

would not have attracted as many top-flight graduate students as it did. The importance of this assistance can be gauged from the fact that 60 per cent of the students replying to the Subcommittee questionnaire received fellowship support in the course of their postwar education in Russian studies, despite the existence of the G. I. Bill. Forty per cent of the respondents were married when they began the area program and 10 per cent married while they were in it. An estimated 40 per cent of the students replying either worked part time themselves or were assisted financially by wives who worked.

The question of scholarship and fellowship aid is, of course, a general problem facing all fields of graduate study. In Russian studies, however, it is complicated by the special demands of education in this field. Many area programs require two years of study for the M. A. degree. Full area preparation for the most promising students should embrace command of the language, multidisciplinary work on the area at the M. A. level, a Ph. D. in a discipline, participation in an interdisciplinary research seminar, and some acquaintance with another non-Western area for comparative purposes; all this may require, depending on the previous language and area preparation of the student, up to an additional year and a half of study beyond that usually necessary for a Ph. D. In addition, difficulties in acquiring and using Russian research materials, often involving travel to the few libraries holding such materials, frequently impose a further burden on the graduate student in the Russian field. If able students are to continue to be attracted to Russian studies, it is essential that they be assisted in meeting the additional costs involved in graduate education in this field.

While it is difficult to foresee their effects at this date, the graduate fellowship provisions of the National Defense Education Act and the enlargement of the National Woodrow Wilson Fellowship Program may have important implications for the fellowship problem in Russian studies and for present fellowship programs in this field.

Training of Government Personnel. In addition to the large number of their students who entered the government after graduation, between 1946 and 1956 the graduate programs in Russian studies also trained a small number of people already in government service, who were assigned to the universities for Russian area training by various government agencies. Some projects for the training of government personnel involved only language training, some both language and area study. In some cases, government personnel entered the graduate area programs as regular students, although usually for only one year of a two-year sequence; in others, government students were trained under special contract and by means of separate or supplementary curricula designed to fit their particular needs and training objectives.

The largest number of government personnel trained were from the armed forces, predominantly the Air Force and the Army. The majority of these received only, or primarily, Russian language training, generally under special contract and outside the regular language curricula of the graduate programs. This special language training was customarily intensive and concentrated in nature and often

70

technical or specialized in substance. Two of the largest programs of this type were at Indiana and Syracuse, where Air Force personnel were given language training under special contract.

A few military personnel received both area and language training through the regular curricula of the graduate programs. In a few cases, projects which combined parts of the regular graduate program in Russian studies with specially designed language and area courses were developed to give military personnel training geared to their particular requirements. Columbia's Russian Institute, for example, worked out a Junior Specialist Training Program for the Air Force. Selected enlisted men and officers took the first-year general courses on Russia in five disciplines required of all students at the Russian Institute; in addition, they received special intensive Russian language training, courses and lectures on the Russian area conducted in Russian by Soviet emigré scholars, and a special colloquium dealing with current Soviet problems. The idea of a few classes and lectures conducted in Russian is one that might well be borrowed for the second-year curricula of the regular graduate Russian area programs, particularly as opportunities for study in the Soviet Union develop.

Nonmilitary government personnel prepared in the graduate programs during the last ten years came primarily from the Department of State (approximately thirty-five officers), with a smaller number from other government agencies. They were customarily trained in the regular curricula of the graduate programs, but only for one year and usually with individually tailored course and

71

seminar sequences. In some cases, part of their work was directed study and reading. Some of the nonmilitary government students, on their own initiative, earned credit toward a graduate degree. A few government personnel, both military and civilian, actually received degrees on the area or in a discipline during the course of their training.

The reaction of teachers and administrators in the graduate Russian area programs to the problem of training government personnel, especially on a contract basis, is mixed. A few maintain that government-training contracts are not only in the national interest but also permit the expansion of the graduate program and the acquisition of faculty members and of library and teaching materials which indirectly or at a later time benefit the regular program. In addition, they help to stimulate administrative and student interest in and support for the graduate program. Those who are less enthusiastic concerning government-training contracts point out that the special training usually required, even when it is supported by new funds and staff, inevitably places some additional teaching and administrative burdens on the regular faculty of the program and tends to deflect the program from its normal academic goals. Despite efforts to minimize the impact of the special training called for, teaching in the regular program may suffer and faculty research time may be reduced. Moreover, the critics say, government contracts are ephemeral; just when major effort has been expended and new staff has been hired, the project may be suddenly discontinued, leaving the program overextended and new faculty members stranded.

Some government officials believe that university training of their personnel has not been entirely satisfactory. They maintain that language training in the graduate Russian area programs is often inadequate for the purposes of government students. It is usually not intensive or rapid enough. Emphasis is on a reading command of the language, and facility in speaking and understanding Russian, an important skill for government officials, particularly those serving overseas, is insufficiently developed, according to government critics. As a result of what it believes to be the deficiencies in university language training, the Foreign Service Institute of the Department of State recently decided to provide the bulk of the Russian language training for State Department employees through its own courses and programs. Against this view must be balanced the fact that the type of language training desired by the government is very costly and can seldom be financed by the universities alone.

There is also some dissatisfaction on the part of government officials with the area training provided by the graduate programs on Russia, although less than in regard to language training. Government observers point out that most government personnel cannot be released for long enough to profit from the full two-year curriculum offered by the more intensive programs. Attending for only one year, government students may waste a good deal of time in formalities or irrelevancies and may miss a number of basic or specialized courses which are given only in alternate years or are not offered when the teachers of the courses are on leave. Furthermore, in the opinion of some government critics, area training in the graduate programs has

73

too "academic" a slant and is too heavily research-oriented for the needs of government personnel.

Those in the government concerned with Russian area training would like to see the graduate programs offer government personnel a concentrated curriculum, providing as broad a general survey of the area as is possible in one year. In such a curriculum, emphasis would be placed on contemporary developments and on rapid analysis and evaluation of policy problems rather than on research. Although some government agencies and training officers are considering the possibility of providing area training through their own resources, most government officials would prefer to see the training of government personnel on the Russian area in the hands of the universities. Moreover, although budgetary and personnel restrictions seldom permit protracted area training for someone already in government service, government-training officers would like to see students in the graduate programs who are pointing toward a career in government acquire even more training, in language and in depth in the area, than they have in the past.

Training of Foreign Students and Scholars. Between 1946 and 1956 over two dozen foreign students were educated at the largest graduate programs in Russian studies, primarily at Columbia. Several of these were of Soviet or East European origin, having emigrated to the West during or immediately after the war. Most of this group have become or are in the process of becoming United States citizens and plan to settle in this country. Approximately six Canadians were trained, the majority of whom returned

74

to Canada and entered academic careers. Roughly a dozen students from Western Europe, largely from Britain and France, were prepared. Half a dozen students from non-Western countries, ranging from Indonesia to Israel, were also educated in the graduate programs on Russia.

Almost half of these foreign students were members of or destined for the diplomatic and other government services of their countries. Their own governments usually sponsored and financed their training. In addition, a number of foreign students were educated under fellowships or grants from American foundations, universities, or other private sources. A few senior foreign scholars also benefited from the graduate programs on the Russian area. Occasionally they received some formal training; more often they were associated with the programs informally in a variety of flexible ways and were engaged primarily in research or in research training.

In many cases foreign students and scholars prepared in the Russian area programs returned to their own countries to act as leading government advisors and experts on Soviet affairs or to become the only, or among the few, academic specialists concerned with the study of Russia and the Soviet Union. A challenging and urgent task for the graduate programs on Russia in the years ahead is to endeavor to attract and train more foreign students and scholars, particularly those from Asia and Africa, where, outside of Japan, Russian studies are little developed.

Postdoctoral Study. During the period under review the graduate programs at Harvard and Columbia, with special foundation support for this purpose, and the Ford Founda-

75

tion Foreign Area Training Fellowship Program, provided fellowship opportunities for postdoctoral study of the Russian area to about twenty American scholars. The majority utilized this opportunity to embark on further study and research relating to the Russian area. A few scholars undertook programs designed for certain specific goals: to add Russian area competence to previous specialization in the East European or some other area; to acquire knowledge of an additional discipline in order to apply it to the Russian area; or to add Russian area competence to previously completed discipline specialization outside the Russian field.

At Columbia, postdoctoral study was encouraged through the availability of "senior fellowships." At Harvard, it was developed by associating established scholars in various disciplines with a research center on the area. Such efforts were not always successful, but in several instances very able scholars were attracted to Russian studies, or the skills of promising young specialists on Russia were improved and extended. In the opinion of most observers, opportunities for postdoctoral training, though limited, contributed significantly to strengthening Russian studies during the postwar decade.

Problems and Opportunities of Russian Area Programs. A review of the experience of the Russian area programs in the last ten years reveals certain particularly difficult problems as well as challenging opportunities for the further development and improvement of Russian area training. Most of these issues derive from concepts and practices peculiar to area study. One of the most important is the question of multidisciplinary study of the area, its breadth

76

and depth and the extent to which such study should be required of all students.

At present, the graduate programs on Russia vary widely in their coverage of the area, as measured by the number of disciplinary approaches to the area offered or required, and the depth of study of the area possible in each discipline. The nucleus of most programs is, quite naturally, history and literature, the disciplines which traditionally have been concerned with the area and in which Russian studies in the United States first developed. Almost all programs also include political science courses on the area, most often in government and international relations, less frequently in law, ideology, and political behavior. A majority of the programs now provide work in Soviet economics, although this is a recent development in some cases. In several programs this is still a major deficiency.

Beyond these four disciplines, the range of approaches to the area is extremely limited. Occasional course offerings in geography, sociology, philosophy, anthropology, and fine arts are scattered among several of the programs. But, in conjunction with an area program, advanced work in Russian geography can be undertaken only at Washington, Indiana, and Syracuse; in sociology, only at Harvard; and the record for the other disciplines is even less satisfactory.

In short, little progress has been made in developing an interest in Russia in those disciplines which in the past have devoted little attention to the Russian area and which the Committee on World Area Research singled out in 1947 as needing special emphasis and encouragement in

Russian studies. Efforts in this regard have been made, but with limited results. This is not surprising, however, when one considers the difficulty and length of time involved in building up area study in a particular discipline. In the beginning, only a few teachers and jobs, courses and books are available; yet somehow able individuals have to be attracted to the study of the area in that discipline and prepared in both the area and the discipline. Even if this is accomplished, it still requires a decade or more before those trained begin to have an effect on the field, in terms of their research results and students, and a generation before the discipline as applied to the area becomes rooted in the academic structure. In Russian studies, a beginning has been made, particularly in geography and sociology, but only a beginning. Russian studies in the United States are still far from approaching the scope and comprehensiveness of our study of Western society.

At one time it was believed that the chief difficulty in persuading students to specialize on Russia in the disciplines that devote little attention to the study of Russian problems was the lengthy period of preparation (as a minimum, four to five years) usually required to develop competence in both the discipline and the area. This does not seem to be the case, however, since fellowship opportunities to support this kind of preparation have been made available, with disappointing results.

The root of the problem may rather be the nature of the disciplines involved. Sociology, for example, has been traditionally concerned with the study of American society or with generalized problems of social behavior. Psychology and some forms of anthropology are oriented toward study of man in the abstract. At present there seems too little realization in these disciplines of the importance of Russian and other non-Western data to the development of more universally applicable concepts and theories. In geography, cultural anthropology, and ethnography, it is customary for the scholar to apply his disciplinary skills to problems in a number of different societies and areas, rather than to specialize in any one culture or region. All of these disciplines are therefore inherently less receptive to area-oriented study than are history and literature, which have traditionally been based on area concentration, or even than political science, which is just beginning to find certain values in comparative and area study. As a result, in many of these disciplines and in their representation in university departments, little professional recognition is accorded to Russian specialization, and concentration in the Russian area is not encouraged.

Another important difficulty is that of identifying individuals interested in combining Russian area study with training in one of the disciplines that devote little attention to Russia, and giving them some reasonable expectation of employment at the conclusion of their graduate preparation. If a university or a private or governmental organization interested in employing a scholar with such a combination of skills could be found, an area program might be able to locate and educate someone willing to undertake the necessary preparation. Such an individual could be sought among graduate students beginning an area program who had not yet made a firm disciplinary commit-

79

ment, or among graduate students or established scholars in the discipline who might agree to add competence in the Russian area to their disciplinary competence. This approach, while admittedly difficult, should perhaps be tried; the need to train a few scholars in the disciplines that now largely ignore Russian problems is an urgent one. Knowledge and insights from these disciplines would contribute significantly to the effort to see Russian society as a whole.

The range of disciplinary courses offered on the Russian area is only one measure of the area coverage of the graduate programs. The depth of that coverage is reflected in the number of advanced courses and seminars offered in each discipline, in addition to the general survey or introductory course. A few programs offer little beyond the general course in each discipline taught, and occasional disciplinary seminars or an "area" seminar. The majority of the programs provide at best one or two advanced courses and a seminar in most of the disciplines they offer. Study in depth, comprising several advanced courses and a seminar in as many as four disciplines, is possible in only a few programs. As noted previously, Ph. D. work in the Russian field is possible at no more than one-half of the institutions at which programs in Russian studies are located.

Still another test of the area coverage of the graduate programs in Russian studies is the number of disciplines in the area in which the student is required to take courses. Of the four largest programs, only Columbia, until recently, required a minimum of a one-term course in each of five disciplines. Washington, which formerly required work in each of three disciplines, raised its requirement to five disciplines in 1957, following additions to its faculty in several disciplines. Harvard and California require courses in any three of the disciplines they offer. In practice, the majority of students in these programs have elected all three of their disciplines in the social sciences, with the focus on history or government, and have taken little or no work in Russian literature or geography. Many of the other programs have no special requirements in regard to the number of disciplines in which courses must be taken but work out the student's course schedule according to his background, needs, and interest. Such a procedure does not always ensure broad multidisciplinary coverage of the area for the student. Under present conditions, it is possible for a number of students, a minority but still a substantial number, to complete their study of the Russian area without work in the humanities or in geography.

There is, however, no unanimity on the number of disciplines in which course work should be required to ensure adequate multidisciplinary study. One view is that the student should be required to take a one-term course on the area in each of at least five disciplines—and in even more, if possible. Anything less leads to the weakening and eventual elimination of the multidisciplinary approach and to the emasculation of the quality of area study.

An opposing viewpoint is that it is sufficient to require work in as few as three disciplines as long as they are divided between the social sciences and the humanities and one of them is mastered thoroughly. Some individuals, on the other hand, believe that it is impossible to set precise requirements for multidisciplinary study of the area; con-

81

sequently, they consider it fruitless to debate how many or which disciplines and courses should be included. In their view, all that is required is a dedication to a genuine multi-disciplinary approach, which can then be applied in the light of the resources of the programs and the needs of individual students.

There is general agreement, however, that the core of a Russian area program should include history, language and literature, economics, and political science (defined broadly to include law and international relations). At the same time, other fields are thought to be of almost equal importance, and vigorous efforts to increase the representation in area programs of such disciplines as geography, sociology, philosophy, and fine arts are strongly recommended.

Interdisciplinary Study. Ideally, the area approach involves more than the application of a range of disciplines to the study of a culture; it also demands that these various disciplinary approaches be related to each other in an effort to see the society as a whole. The development of such an integrated, interdisciplinary approach to the study of Russia is one of the most important objectives of Russian area studies.

During the postwar decade the graduate programs in Russian studies endeavored to achieve this objective in a variety of ways. Almost all of them failed. The methods most commonly utilized were required sequences of related courses, "core" courses, comprehensive written or oral examinations on the area as a whole, multidisciplinary or "area" seminars, and group or coordinated research.

Course sequences provide only a multidisciplinary approach; "core" courses tend toward a single or, at best, a double disciplinary outlook; comprehensive examinations are generally a series of disciplinary questions grouped together at one time and place; "area" seminars are often made up of specialized disciplinary papers and discussions presented seriatim; and group or coordinated research has proved difficult in conception and organization.

Of the four largest graduate-training programs, Harvard and Washington require special comprehensive examinations on the area. Three also attempt to achieve an interdisciplinary approach through required group or joint seminars, two of the research type (at Columbia and Washington), one of the discussion variety (at Harvard).

Only two instances were found in which progress in interdisciplinary study had reportedly been made. In both cases, those involved were advanced graduate students, young teachers, and senior scholars. Students beginning area study did not participate. This suggests that interdisciplinary study is possible only after a multidisciplinary knowledge of the area has been acquired, some command of and practice in a disciplinary skill has been developed, and some reflection and maturing of judgment has occurred.

At the University of Washington interdisciplinary study was stimulated through a coordinated research project on "Russia in Asia," in which faculty members and predoctoral students from several disciplines participated. No attempt was made to train students to do research in disciplines other than their own, but each member of the research seminar was expected to state and define his

83

problem in terms of its relationship to other problems and other approaches represented in the seminar. In addition, he could observe and comment on the research presentations of the other disciplines, and he had his own work criticized from various disciplinary points of view. In the process he learned a good deal about the techniques and insights of the other disciplines, and his own research was correspondingly broadened and improved. He was not told about interdisciplinary values; he actually experienced them—in the organization and criticism of his own work and by examining critically research results from other disciplines.

Several devices helped to promote interdisciplinary study at the Russian Research Center of Harvard University. Scholars and graduate students from several disciplines engaged in cooperative research, joined in discussion seminars or meetings, and, most important, according to some members of the Center, studied in close physical proximity to each other and ate lunch together regularly at the Center. As a result of these activities, the individuals concerned had frequent informal opportunities to exchange ideas and learn something of the concepts and techniques of other disciplines, thereby broadening their own approach to the area.

Part of the difficulty in developing interdisciplinary study may stem from confusion over its definition—what it is and what it can be expected to achieve. If it is defined as the mastery of more than one discipline or the ability to use other disciplines as analytical tools, this is extremely difficult and is seldom achieved. If it is defined more modestly, however, as an attempt to make the student aware of the information, insights, and approaches which other disciplines can contribute to an understanding of the area as a whole and often to individual problems in the study of Russian and Soviet society, the objecive should be within reach.

The need for an interdisciplinary approach in Russian studies rests to a considerable degree on the realization that our knowledge of Russia is still limited in comparison with that of our own Western culture. For example, students learning about West European governments bring to such a study a wide background of knowledge. They have learned much about the literature, history, and traditions of Western Europe from their undergraduate and even secondary education. In disciplines in which they may have little training, such as economics or philosophy, there are numerous well-reasoned treatises and manuals in English which will guide their studies. A number of theoretical approaches to Western society, the result of a generation or more of thought and discussion, provide them with alternative frames of reference and stimulate them to formulate their own concepts.

In the case of Russian studies, the student has no such educational background and body of information on which to draw. In many cases, his teachers have been working in the field for only a few years, and nothing comparable to the vast accumulation of knowledge about Western society is available to him. There is, of course, much to be said for interdisciplinary study even as applied to Western culture, where the compartmentalization of disciplines frequently serves as an obstacle to progress and understanding. In the study of Russia and other non-Western areas, how-

ever, it is an essential instrument for increasing our understanding of these societies. Through interdisciplinary study
a frame of reference can be developed which is not based
wholly on assumptions derived from Western experience
and to which specialized work, otherwise isolated in its
approach and results and more or less lost in the wilderness
of general ignorance, can be related.

In attempting to foster an interdisciplinary point of view
among students, one of the most promising approaches is
through coordinated research around a common topic.
Where skills and information from various disciplines are
focused on related aspects of a single problem, an interdisciplinary effect is more likely to be produced. This was
often the case in government research and analysis relating
to Russia during the war; the outcome of scholarly conferences in recent years on continuity and change in Russian and Soviet thought and on the transformation of Russian society, and the experience of the "Russia in Asia"
research project at the University of Washington, also
seem to bear this out.

It is generally agreed that each student must develop an
interdisciplinary outlook for himself. Nevertheless, it is
possible to stimulate and assist this process in ways such as
those described above. It is important, therefore, that the
Russian area programs support coordinated research seminars and other projects designed to prepare the ground for
the maturation of an interdisciplinary attitude in the student.

Comparative Area Study. In many respects comparative
study of other areas or coordinated study of problems in

more than one area is a logical extension of interdisciplinary study of a single area. During the last few years interest in inter-area study has been growing among those concerned with Russian studies. Washington, whose Russian area program is closely related to its Far Eastern program, has evolved some inter-area study techniques of promise and is in the process of developing an extension of cooperative and comparative area research. Columbia has undertaken an interesting experiment in inter-area research training. Faculty members and students specializing in foreign-policy problems in both the Russian and Far Eastern area programs meet together in one seminar to discuss research papers dealing with various aspects of Soviet-Far Eastern relations. Russian area programs associated with East European programs also possess considerable potential for the development of useful comparative study and inter-area research.

Much benefit could be derived from the sharing of information and experience among scholars concerned with the different countries of the Soviet bloc, and the development of such cooperation should be a major objective of Russian studies in the coming decade. Through coordinated research, comparative studies of analogous problems, and analyses of diplomatic, party, and economic relationships, fresh insights concerning individual areas in the Soviet orbit could be developed, and the range of knowledge concerning problems common to all socialist societies could be extended.

Much has been learned about the Russian area by comparison and contrast with the West, but this juxtaposition alone has serious dangers. One of the underlying short-comings of Western thinking about Russia has been the assumption that Russia is following the same path of development as Western societies but is somewhat retarded and maladjusted. The possibility that Russia as a fully modernized society may be as different from the West as is its heritage has not been given sufficient consideration. One means of getting away from this Western-oriented approach to Russia is to develop the comparative study of Russian and other cultures—Arabic, Chinese, Japanese, Indian. The steps in this direction that have recently been taken in universities having area programs dealing with several cultures promise to produce valuable results.

As a factor in graduate education on the Russian area, the comparative study approach requires that students take a few courses dealing with a second area and participate in research seminars that are both interdisciplinary and inter-area. While comparative area studies are clearly of limited applicability at the training level—although a few exceptional students have acquired real competence on both Russia and another area in the postwar decade—they can nevertheless contribute much to the theoretical approach of the student. At the research level, there is reason to hope that comparative area studies conducted systematically over a period of time will provide a much sounder perspective for the study of any given area.

Period Coverage of Russian Area Study. Another important issue in Russian area study that has aroused much discussion is the relative emphasis that should be placed on pre-Soviet as opposed to Soviet developments. Some observers point out that prior to World War II most of the limited education and research in Russian studies dealt with the pre-1917 period, and that the Soviet Union was relatively little studied. One of the objectives of the postwar programs was to redress this balance by subjecting the Soviet period to particularly careful scrutiny. In this effort, there was no intention to neglect the study of pre-1917 Russia, which was considered indispensable to an understanding of the Soviet Union. Moreover, it is pointed out, in most of the postwar graduate programs, a number of courses and a considerable amount of research have treated Russia before the revolution.

Others concerned with Russian studies believe that, with the best of intentions, the postwar area programs could not help but be influenced by the general atmosphere current in the period of their founding and early development. In the years immediately following World War II there was an urgent national need to learn as much as possible concerning Soviet developments and to have a number of Americans competent in this area. In the opinion of some observers, the graduate area programs did their best in this situation to eschew a contemporary approach to the study of Russia and to keep a balanced emphasis between Tsarist and Soviet periods in their education and research. Nevertheless, student and public interest and the pressure of events generated an atmosphere which led to greater concentration on the Soviet period. In most programs more courses dealt with the Soviet system than with modern Russia as a whole; courses treating the earlier period were generally found only in history and literature.

89

Consequently, the programs often tended to be oriented toward recent and even contemporary events, and many students learned relatively little about Russia's past.

In regard to the future focus of Russian area study, there is general agreement that it is not a question of studying either the Soviet era or Russia before 1917: both must be included. Most students and scholars believe that an understanding of the Soviet Union depends to a considerable degree on a thorough knowledge of its historical, cultural, and institutional antecedents. Many also feel that the Russian area deserves serious study not only because of its present importance but because its history and civilization represent a significant part of human experience, providing perspective and comparative insights for an understanding of our own and Western European society. The question then is one of emphasis, selection, and method; in even the extended amount of time required for area training, there are only a limited number of courses and seminars the student can take. How best can his time be allocated?

Naturally, much depends on the student's background, disciplinary interest, and objectives. This suggests the need for considerable flexibility in program requirements. Even so, there should probably be certain general goals for all students. One solution would be to retain the emphasis on the Soviet period now common to most courses in economics, political science, and sociology but to place specific responsibility for the necessary general background to this work on courses in history and literature. Such courses would be, in a sense, "core" courses, designed to provide the student with a multidisciplinary understanding of Russia's past, including the development of political and economic institutions, social structure, and intellectual and cultural currents. These courses would be required of all students as preparation for study of the Soviet system itself.

The emphasis in such background work might well be on the period of the modernization of Russia, including the evolution of modern political institutions, industrialization, social changes, contact with the West, revolutionary movements, and intellectual developments. In such an approach comparative analysis of the emergence of Russian institutions, particularly in relation to despotism, agricultural change, social structure, and industrialization, should be included.

Field Experience and Travel. For the greater part of the postwar decade, the Soviet Union was inaccessible as a result of restrictions on travel and the exchange of persons imposed by the Soviet government. This was a major handicap for graduate education in Russian studies and forced heavy reliance on intensive and highly developed methods of area training. Although there could be no real substitute for first-hand experience in Russia, this handicap was compensated for, by dint of imagination and hard work, as effectively as circumstances permitted. In addition, a few students acquired indirect field experience by visiting Yugoslavia or working in research libraries in Finland and other parts of Europe.

In 1954-55 the Soviet government began granting visas for trips to Russia of thirty days' duration, and the Inter-University Committee on Travel Grants, with assistance

91

from the foundations, helped to finance scholars in Russian and East European studies on such trips. During the succeeding three years approximately one hundred and fifty scholars visited the area for brief periods of travel and study. It is much to the credit of the graduate programs that all students replying to the Subcommitee questionnaire who had visited the Soviet Union believed that their preparation in the programs had admirably equipped them for this experience. Under the terms of the 1958 cultural-exchange agreement between the United States and Soviet governments, twenty-two American graduate students in Russian studies attended Moscow and Leningrad universities during the academic year 1958-59, and seventeen Soviet graduate students attended several American universities. It is expected that this exchange and others, such as those of undergraduate and graduate students conducted for brief periods in the summers of 1958 and 1959, will be continued and expanded in the years ahead. Exchanges of scholars and teachers may also be initiated.

The growing accessibility of the Soviet Union is one of the most encouraging prospects and important challenges for Russian studies in the United States. If it becomes possible for a substantial number of students and scholars to study and do research in the U.S.S.R., this will have a profound effect on graduate education in Russian studies. Present graduate programs and training methods are based largely on an assumption of inability to work in the area and study it directly. Curricula, readings, the intensity of the work load, language training, and the selection of research topics have all been shaped accordingly and will have to be recast in some degree if study and research in the Soviet Union become possible for any number of students.

Language training would probably benefit most immediately and directly from increased accessibility to Russia. Students would be expected to acquire a basic command of Russian before proceeding to the area, but the development of real competence and fluency, particularly in speaking and understanding Russian, would be immeasurably accelerated by immersion in the area for six months or longer. Such an opportunity would be particularly advantageous for the student of Russian literature, who must know the language not simply as a set of symbols with equivalent meanings but must have the "feel" of the language, recognizing idioms and usage, the overtones and associations of words, and differences in levels of speech.

If the Soviet Union is generally opened for study and research, the reorganization of graduate education in Russian studies will have to be considered as a general problem, involving not only language training but other broad issues: for example, the amount of preparatory work needed in the United States before going to the area, the optimum time to remain in the U.S.S.R., the accrediting by American universities of work done at Soviet institutions, and ways for coordinating and guiding research carried out in the Soviet Union. At the same time each discipline and each student will have to be considered on an individual basis. For example, the benefits to be derived from study in the U.S.S.R. will undoubtedly be smaller in ideology and politics than in literature or geography. Similarly, the background, capabilities, and interests of students will be factors in determining how experience in the area will best complement their graduate preparation.

Thus, it seems likely that study and travel in the U.S.S.R., as a part of graduate education in Russian studies, will have to be developed on a flexible basis. In some cases, a specially designed program of preparatory study combined with extended residence in the Soviet Union will prove to be most effective; in others, the graduate programs in the United States will still have to provide most of the training, followed by briefer visits to the area. Ways should also be devised to utilize the presence at American universities of Soviet students and scholars in the education of American students on Russia. In general, it is important that those directing Russian studies programs should consider imaginatively the effect that the development of contacts and exchanges with the Soviet Union may have on their present efforts in education and research.

Teaching Methods. Many observers believe that, in addition to the potentialities of growing contacts with the Soviet Union, the Russian area programs have a special opportunity and responsibility to develop modern and ground-breaking methods of graduate instruction. In this view, the programs in Russian studies, blessed with small cohesive groups of highly motivated students, all engaged in sharply defined courses of work, should undertake controlled experiments designed to test novel and unusual graduate-teaching techniques. There is now considerable dissatisfaction on the part of both students and teachers with the teaching methods used in the graduate Russian area programs. While some of the criticisms voiced are applicable to graduate education in general, others seem to be particularly pertinent to Russian area study, where intensive and difficult specialized work is being offered a small number of able students.

The chief complaints are: (1) too much of the work is given in the form of large lecture courses, both of a survey nature and even on specialized subjects—consequently, there is almost no opportunity for discussion; (2) the survey courses in the various disciplines often overlap each other and appear uncoordinated in their approach; (3) contact with and guidance from the faculty are minimal, even in seminar work; (4) little systematic help is provided in the location and use of sources and reference materials and in general research techniques; (5) the work load is often so heavy that no time is left for individual study and reflection or for other than required reading; and (6) no training or preparation for teaching is provided.

Some of the suggestions for improvement that have been made are based on the assumption, discussed earlier in the chapter, that in the future more students will enter the graduate programs with some prior knowledge of the Russian area. If this turns out to be the case, it would make possible such curricular changes as the substitution of discussion classes based on a fundamental list of readings for survey lecture courses in each discipline. It might also make feasible an increase in the number of disciplinary approaches to the area that can be encompassed in the already heavy schedule of the area student. For example, a student with considerable background study of Russian history might be able to plunge directly into special lecture courses, colloquia, or seminars in that field, with a course or discussion class in another discipline replacing the survey of Russian history he would normally be required to take. In almost every case, smaller classes, more opportunity for discussion, and closer student-faculty contact would substantially improve the instruction offered in the area programs.

Structure and Organization of Area Programs. Russian area programs, as well as general Slavic and East European programs which include the Russian area, are now organized in diverse ways. The majority take the form of an interdepartmental faculty committee, whose chairman is usually the chief adviser to students taking graduate work in the Russian area. The committee in one or two cases has its own office or seminar room and a small budget, but is more often without separate funds or a special position in the university. The chief functions of the committee are to develop and maintain liaison and cooperation with the discipline departments, to determine which departmental courses shall be included in the offerings of the program, and to establish the requirements for and certify the granting of Russian area degrees, when the program offers such degrees. The chairman and members of the committee are almost always regular members of discipline departments. The extent to which they can, individually or collectively, exert pressure on departments, departmental chairmen, and the university administration varies widely, depending on the personality and initiative of the chairman and committee members and on the particular university situation.

The programs at California and Columbia are organized

as semiautonomous institutes within the university framework; at Washington the program is part of such an institute. At Washington the institute is a separate entity; at California and Columbia the institutes are related to an area study or international relations "umbrella" organization or "holding company" in the university. Several committee-organized programs are similarly related to a central body.

The institute director or chairman is usually rooted in a discipline department of the university, but part of his time is released for the administration of the institute. This time is generally paid for by the institute, occasionally by the department. Most often the institute faculty are regular members of discipline departments, paid from the departmental budgets. In a few cases, individuals on the institute staff are paid by and work for the institute alone or are shared, in time and salary, by the institute and a department. Frequently, when the institute pays for all or part of a man's time, this is done in order to acquire an individual not otherwise obtainable because of an initial lack of interest in him on the part of the department or because of a shortage of departmental funds. Such a man, if he proves acceptable to the department and the university, is usually transferred to the departmental budget after a few years.

The institutes customarily have separate budgets and physical facilities. The budget may cover some or all of the following items: administrative time of the director, secretarial and office expenses, library support, research (acquisition of materials, research assistantships, released time from teaching for institute faculty), publications,

97

scholarships and fellowships, and "pump-priming" to acquire new staff, as described above. In some cases, a large part of this budget is provided by foundation grants. On the other hand, the university generally bears the major costs of instruction.

There is substantial agreement on certain prerequisites for a full-fledged graduate program on the Russian area. In addition to a language program, it is considered desirable to have mature scholars primarily concerned with graduate teaching in Russian studies in at least five of the major disciplines. Most observers also believe that graduate programs, especially when they embrace research programs, should have a semiautonomous organization and budget, and formal recognition in the university catalog, while maintaining close liaison with the discipline departments and having their teaching staff based there. Even in the cases where training and research are separately organized, it is important that the training program should possess sufficient status to permit it to negotiate effectively with the discipline departments concerning new appointments, faculty research time, and other matters of mutual concern. In several institutions, both the preservation of some autonomy and the promotion of cooperation with the discipline departments have been facilitated by the existence of a central organization embracing several area programs.

It should be recognized that full-fledged Russian area programs are very costly. It is probably fair to estimate the average annual budget for a large program as approaching $150,000, including salaries, and library, research, and overhead expenses. Scholarship and general funds provided under the National Defense Education Act may be of some assistance in helping those universities with the extensive scholarly resources necessary to support full-fledged Russian area programs to meet the heavy costs involved, but some additional assistance from outside the university will also be necessary if the fullest potential of the programs in education and research is to be reached.

There is some feeling that, when Russian area programs are a part of general East European or Slavic programs, separate preparation on both Russia and Eastern Europe should be provided, and the primary area interest and responsibility of each student should be clearly defined. As long as offerings on each area in five disciplines are available, this can often be done through the setting of precise requirements for the completion of training in each area; and it does not necessarily involve the separation of the Russian and East European programs, whose close relationship may, in fact, provide certain advantages for comparative study and inter-area research. There is some danger, however, that in joint Russian-East European programs the lines of distinction between training in each area may become blurred. When this happens, the programs may well not be giving the student adequate preparation in either area. Instead, he emerges with a smattering of knowledge concerning both areas but without full competence in either.

During the last decade the various graduate programs concerned with Russia did very little to coordinate their efforts. Some cooperation on projects in the library field was developed, but in training, each program went more or less its own way. In a few cases, a program emphasized one aspect, period, or discipline in its training, but this arose by chance or historical accident, not from any conscious division of labor. When some coordination of effort did occur, it took the form of careful guidance and counseling to students. Those with special interests were advised to begin or continue their graduate education in Russian studies at other universities especially qualified to satisfy those interests. In the last few years interest in avoiding duplication of effort and in a division of labor regarding acquisitions, research, and training has been growing, certainly a hopeful sign for the future.

Library Resources. An essential function of the graduate area programs is that of fostering research. This is particularly important in a field such as Russian studies, where so many problems remain to be investigated. Participation in research projects sponsored by the area programs also provides valuable training for advanced graduate students. The central feature of a research program is a body of scholars engaged in individual or group projects. The scholars normally come both from the home institution, where they are temporarily released from all or part of their teaching duties, and from other institutions in a visiting capacity. An important aid to research, as well as to teaching, for graduate students and scholars in the Russian area programs during the last decade has been the *Current Digest of the Soviet Press*, sponsored by the Joint Committee on Slavic Studies, with generous foundation assistance. This weekly collection of translated articles and summaries from Soviet newspapers and journals serves not only the world of scholarship but also reaches government officials, journalists, and many others interested in Soviet affairs.

Emphasis on research can be effective only when an institution has substantial library resources. In view of the wide variety of possible research topics, it is difficult to generalize as to the library holdings that are desirable. As a rough rule of thumb, however, it seems reasonable to suggest that for research purposes a library should have Russian language holdings of not fewer than 20,000 volumes, and an annual budget of not less than $10,000 for the purchase of Russian language books.

Special Programs. Most of the issues discussed in the preceding pages relate to things the area programs did during the last ten years and to problems with which scholars and administrators in Russian studies are familiar. During the next decade the graduate programs will face new challenges and unfamiliar problems arising from the growing interest in the study of Russia in American colleges and secondary schools. To sustain and to develop this interest, more teachers knowledgeable about Russia are needed.

One way quickly to increase the supply of such teachers is for the graduate programs in Russian studies to provide special training for established college teachers who wish to add competence in the Russian area to their previously acquired disciplinary skill. There are a number of teachers in American colleges who, because of their own interest or at the request of their departments, are teaching courses

101

dealing wholly or in part with the Russian area, although they lack formal training in Russian studies. There are also a number of teachers who are interested in the area but who have not had an opportunity either to study it or to teach it. The graduate programs in Russian studies can help to meet the needs of such individuals by developing and supervising special courses of study for them. These will have to be devised flexibly, taking account of institutional and individual needs in each case. Such programs might range from one or two summers of intensive work to fifteen months of study (two summers and an academic year). The teachers involved might take many of the basic courses offered in the regular area program, in addition to special colloquia or seminars dealing with their field of interest and with the problems of undergraduate instruction in Russian studies.[9]

Another type of special program of importance to the graduate Russian area programs is the summer language institute, such as those developed at Middlebury College and Indiana University. Summer language institutes provide an opportunity for students planning to embark on graduate study of the Russian area to begin or advance their language training prior to the opening of graduate school. Intermediate and advanced students also have a chance to develop greater fluency in speaking and understanding Russian. Summer language programs therefore

9. A fuller discussion of this and other ways in which the graduate programs on Russia can support and assist the development of Russian studies in undergraduate education will be found in the succeeding chapter, particularly pp. 144-51.

form an important supplement to the language training provided in the regular area programs. With the encouragement offered by the National Defense Education Act, more summer language institutes should be developed in the next few years, and area students should be urged to utilize them for the development and refinement of language skills.

A special summer program combining the development of language facility with additional area training and indirect contact with the area was conducted in 1958 under the supervision of the Institute for the Study of the U.S.S.R. A summer seminar was held at its headquarters in Munich, in which graduate students and young instructors in Russian studies from a variety of countries participated. The lectures and discussion were led by émigré Soviet scholars connected with the Institute and were conducted primarily in Russian. The subject matter was selected to meet the interests of a broad range of students; at the same time the students were encouraged to initiate or continue their own research projects on the area, making use of the valuable library at the Institute. This type of program promises to be a useful addition to the supplementary resources available for graduate education in Russian studies.

VI

Graduate Education in a Single Discipline with Specialization on Russia. Between 1946 and 1957 some students educated in Russian studies were prepared not in the multidisciplinary area programs but through traditional methods of graduate study, i.e., in a single discipline with specialization on Russia. As noted previously, during the postwar decade about thirty students attending universities with graduate Russian area programs proceeded directly to a Ph. D. in a discipline with Russian specialization, without undertaking an area program. A few students acquired Ph. D.'s through specialization on Russia in a single discipline at universities not offering graduate programs on the Russian area. In addition, an indeterminate number of students, both at universities having area programs and at other universities, received an M. A. in a discipline with Russian specialization but did not go through an area program.

During the coming decade education in Russian studies through specialization on Russia in a single discipline should grow. Students educated in this fashion will help meet the expected increased demand for undergraduate teachers in Russian studies. While these students will not receive as complete preparation as those in the area programs, and their number will undoubtedly be smaller, it is important that the objectives and standards of this pattern of education be clearly defined and maintained at the highest possible level.

Graduate education in Russian studies through work in a single discipline is in accord with certain realities in the Russian field. In the first place, a full-fledged area program requires very extensive resources in faculty, course offerings, library facilities, and funds (as noted in the preceding section, some of the requirements are mature scholars offering graduate work on Russia in at least five disciplines, annual Russian-language library acquisitions of $10,000, and a total annual budget approaching $150,000). Only a limited number of institutions have resources of this kind, and they can be developed elsewhere only slowly. Some other institutions, however, possess important resources in Russian studies; while these do not meet the above standards and are not adequate to support a complete area program, they can be utilized to provide excellent preparation on Russia in each of two or three disciplines. It is essential that these institutions undertake educational programs in Russian studies that accord with their capacities; they should not attempt to offer a type of preparation that they are not equipped to give.

Secondly, many of the approximately eighteen hundred undergraduate institutions in the country may want to add courses in the Russian field during the coming decade. The area programs alone will probably not be able to meet the demand for undergraduate teachers prepared to offer such courses. At the same time the colleges will not necessarily prefer the highly specialized graduate of the area program for such teaching positions; they will undoubtedly be equally willing to employ an individual with broad disciplinary preparation, including specialization in the Russian aspect of the discipline.

A further consideration is that a number of students may prefer a general grounding in the area, primarily in their discipline, to the highly specialized preparation called for in the full multidisciplinary area program. They may, for example, be interested primarily in the comparative aspects of the Russian data in their field. Students interested in undergraduate teaching may wish only to include in their general disciplinary preparation sufficient work on Russia to equip them to teach a comparative or special course dealing with the Russian aspect of their discipline. Other students may not want to invest the added time and effort that full area study requires.

Graduate education in Russian studies through specialization on Russia in a single discipline is, of course, less demanding than preparation in an area program. There are, however, certain basic requirements for this pattern of education in Russian studies. Students preparing themselves in this fashion,should have command of the Russian language, as well as of French or German, and training in their discipline equivalent to that received by other graduate students in the discipline. They should also be advised and encouraged to take as many courses on Russia in other disciplines as possible. The extent to which they can study the Russian aspects of disciplines other than their own will depend on the availability of such courses in the university and the demands of their own programs in the major discipline. Students specializing in the Russian aspects of a single discipline should naturally do as much reading as possible on Russia in their own discipline; they should also write their dissertations on topics in the Russian field or on subjects which draw on comparative materials from the Russian experience.

As with Russian area programs, graduate education through specialization on Russia in a single discipline requires certain minimum library resources. Since students are expected to do original research in the Russian field, sufficient materials to permit this must be on hand or easily available. At the same time students should be encouraged to travel to major repositories of Russian materials outside the university to gather additional information for their dissertations. While it is not possible to set exact quantitative standards for library resources in universities offering discipline specialization on Russia, it can be stated that adequate materials for reading and research should be available in each discipline in which graduate work on Russia is given. The level of resources necessary will, of course, be somewhat lower if the institution is in the vicinity of a library with substantial holdings in the Russian field.

It is expected that the majority of students specializing on Russia in a single discipline will go into undergraduate teaching. In the colleges the bulk of their teaching will undoubtedly be in general aspects of their discipline, and they must therefore be well prepared in their disciplinary field. At the same time they will almost certainly have opportunities to use their knowledge of Russia to good advantage. They will be well prepared to inject comparative and other materials on Russia into general courses in the discipline in which they teach. They may be able to offer a comparative course in their field, in which Russian developments would play a significant role. Or, in a growing number of institutions, they will probably be asked to teach a course dealing specifically with Russia.

Whatever their exact contribution to the curriculum, it seems likely that individuals well prepared on Russia in a single discipline will also serve to stimulate general interest in Russian studies among both faculty and students. They will bring with them from graduate school enthusiasm and knowledge concerning Russia; in many instances, they will undoubtedly have a significant effect on the intellectual climate of their teaching institutions and of the surrounding community.

In addition to preparing undergraduate teachers through specialization on Russia in a single discipline, graduate schools with some resources in Russian studies can provide very useful services designed to help meet the growing demand in American communities for more knowledge about Russia and the Communist orbit. As a result of the burgeoning interest in Russian studies in secondary schools, a number of social studies teachers are anxious to learn about the Russian area; they want to provide their students with accurate information concerning the Soviet Union and Communist societies in general. Graduate institutions, in cooperation with schools of education and professional organizations in the educational field, should therefore undertake to provide educational opportunities in Russian studies for secondary-school teachers.

A variety of approaches might be tried. One would be the establishment of brief institutes or workshops on Russia and the Soviet Union. These might take the form of a series of weekend conferences, of intensive one-week sessions between semesters, or of six-week programs in the summer. Programs of this kind would be designed primarily to offer a brief survey of the Russian area to individuals who did not want to become specialists on Russia but who would like to know more about the area. Participants might include, in addition to secondary-school teachers, college students acquiring summer credits, journalists, community leaders, and curious citizens from various walks of life. Several graduate programs on the Russian area have already experimented with institutes of this type. The University of Washington has sponsored on several occasions brief institutes on Russia built around a series of lectures and discussions. The University of Michigan has offered a summer program on the Soviet Union for several years in conjunction with its regular summer school. Courses on Russia in several disciplines are given as part of the summer-school offerings; in addition, a special interdepartmental survey of Soviet problems is offered, and coordinating and advisory services are provided for those participating in the program. The interdepartmental course has been so successful that it is now being given as an undergraduate offering available in the regular academic year, as well as through the extension program of the university.

Working together with members of the school of education and with the social studies teachers themselves, graduate institutions with resources in Russian studies should also provide consulting services to the elementary and secondary schools in their regions. In addition, study materials on Russia useful for teachers and their students need to be developed and tried out. The University of Wisconsin and Michigan State University are already planning general projects to include services of this type.

109

At Michigan State institutes and workshops are also envisaged.[10] As experience with the problems of assisting secondary-school teachers interested in Russian studies develops, other approaches will undoubtedly emerge.

The success of programs of this kind will depend to a large degree on local initiative and planning. The Russian specialists in the graduate schools will need the advice and assistance of secondary-school teachers, professional educators, and others concerned with problems in public- and private-school instruction. Through such cooperation significant centers of influence for the development of Russian studies in various geographical regions of the country can be built up.

VII

Russian Studies in General Graduate Education. Up to this point we have concentrated on the problems and opportunities confronting graduate education on Russia in those universities with Russian area programs or with considerable resources in Russian studies. This is appropriate, since the study of Russia in the coming decade will be carried on largely at such institutions. But, in fact, only a very few universities now have the resources to support a Russian area program, and perhaps a dozen are able to offer specialization on Russia at the Ph. D. level in one or more individual disciplines. Over the next decade this figure can be

10. See Chapter 3 for further discussion of these and other ways in which the graduate schools can help to meet the demand for more study of Russia in American schools.

increased only gradually. What, then, of the many other graduate schools which are preparing secondary-school and college teachers at the M. A. and Ph. D. levels? What should their role be in developing and expanding the study of Russia in American education?

If one accepts the assumptions set forth in our earlier discussion of the growing significance of Russian studies— that the Russian language is rapidly becoming a world language in the sciences and other fields, and that every educated American should know something about Communism and the Soviet system—then it is clear that every graduate institution has an important contribution to make. The functions and responsibilities that the majority of graduate schools can undertake are more limited and less demanding than those of the few universities which possess specialized resources in Russian studies, but they are no less essential to the over-all objectives of Russian studies. Their brief treatment in this paper is a measure, not of their significance, but of their complexity.

In helping to raise the level of American knowledge and understanding regarding Russia and the Soviet orbit, the first task of the graduate schools is to make available to all graduate students, whether in the social sciences and humanities, or in the natural sciences and technical fields, adequate instruction in the Russian language as a practical research tool. In some universities and disciplines, Russian is already becoming a normal equivalent to French or German for meeting graduate language requirements.

As the following chapters suggest, there is every expectation that a rapidly growing number of American colleges

111

and secondary schools will offer instruction in the Russian language in the decade ahead. As a result, more students will be entering graduate school with some knowledge of Russian. There will still be many, however, who either will have had no opportunity to study Russian previously, or who will only decide that they need or want to know Russian late in their undergraduate years or when they reach graduate school. For all such students, the graduate schools should make available, either through their own resources or by drawing upon the offerings of the undergraduate colleges in their universities, enough instruction in the Russian language to provide a working command of the language. This means, for the student who knows no Russian, at least a three-year sequence of study, or its equivalent in intensive courses, and requires that the university have enough teachers and course offerings to support a Russian language program of this extent. The utility of "scientific Russian" courses is a matter of some debate among language teachers themselves, and depends to a considerable degree on the way such a course is taught and on the needs and abilities of the students involved. Almost all observers agree, however, on the value of intensive language instruction, although this requires a fairly large proportion of the graduate student's time to achieve maximum effectiveness.

A second important step for the graduate schools is to offer students in the social sciences and humanities comparative or special courses dealing with Russia in as many disciplines as possible. As more teachers are prepared in Russian studies, it should be possible to have such courses taught by instructors who have been educated in the Russian area programs or who have specialized on Russia in their discipline. Readings, however, should be primarily in English and West European languages, and a wide range of graduate students should be encouraged to take the courses. The university can do much in this way to broaden the preparation and outlook of graduate students undertaking traditional discipline study, which is now so heavily oriented toward American and West European problems.

In addition, some universities, though not in a position to offer specialization on Russia at the Ph. D. level in any discipline, should be able to develop sufficient staff educated in Russian studies and enough special or comparative courses dealing with Russia to permit graduate students to offer the Russian or Soviet aspect of their discipline as a minor field for the Ph. D. general examinations. In this way students could be encouraged and prepared to include the Russian aspect of their discipline in their general undergraduate teaching.

If every American graduate school made available instruction in the Russian language and as many as possible offered some course work on Russia, this would soon have a significant effect on American graduate education as a whole. The result would be a substantial contribution to efforts to extend the horizon of our study of the modern world and to raise the general level of American knowledge and sophistication concerning the Soviet Union and the Communist system.

113

2

Russia and Other Non-Western
Areas in Undergraduate Education

ROBERT F. BYRNES & JOHN M. THOMPSON

AMERICAN[1] education at all levels is under constant review by teachers, students, parents, and interested citizens. Scrutiny of higher education has been especially intense in recent years because of the steadily rising percentage of a rapidly growing population which attends college; because of the scientific, technical, social, and political revolutions through which we and other peoples of the world are passing; and because of the challenge to our institutions and values posed by Communism and the Communist state system dominated by the Soviet Union. These analyses have fluctuated, with interest high during one period in the sciences, in another period in foreign languages, in a third period in some other aspect of American education. However, since the end of the Second World War in

1. This paper is based on a pilot study of the attention devoted to non-Western areas in undergraduate education in the state of Indiana and on the discussion at a conference on this subject held at Indiana Uni-

particular, when the United States was forced to accept large international responsibilities, many Americans have been especially concerned about the effectiveness with which our schools and colleges are preparing our students—the average as well as the academically talented— for life in a shrinking world where our obligations and interests are inevitably becoming ever more connected with those of other peoples.

Many thoughtful citizens, in examining the relevancy of our education for life in the second half of the twentieth century, have become convinced that developments in science and international affairs make necessary a radical departure from established procedures. In particular they have come to believe that our educational system does not pay sufficient attention to the history, intellectual activity, patterns of culture, and interests of peoples living outside the Americas and Western Europe. They demand, along with President Cornelis W. de Kiewiet, of the University

versity, September 18-20, 1958. The papers presented at this conference have been published in Robert F. Byrnes, ed., *The Non-Western Areas in Undergraduate Education in Indiana* (Bloomington: Indiana University Publications, Slavic and East European Series, Vol. XV, 1959).

In this article, "non-Western" does not have cultural connotations but simply designates those areas of the world whose study has been largely neglected in the traditional curricula of American education, i.e., all the areas of the world except that part of Europe not under Communist rule, and the Western hemisphere.

The authors gratefully acknowledge the assistance of Mr. Robert Feldman and Mr. Matthew Downey in the preparation of this report. They also wish to express their appreciation to the presidents, deans, and faculty members of the Indiana colleges and universities for their friendly cooperation and enthusiastic interest in this study.

of Rochester, that we attain the "pervading awareness throughout the total body of the curriculum of the great transformations in the modern world which have the cumulative effect of producing the greatest crisis in human history."

The United States has an extraordinary variety of institutions of higher education—large and small, rich and poor, urban and rural, state and private, liberal and technical and professional, religious and secular, old and new, good and bad. Consequently, while many know well one institution, or a few institutions, no one can speak with accuracy concerning American education in general and the kind of information and understanding it provides concerning other peoples in particular. The state of Indiana was therefore selected as a sample state, and a pilot study of undergraduate education in Indiana was completed in the spring and early summer of 1958. We consider the Indiana sample fairly representative of American higher education in general, although Indiana probably has a slightly higher percentage of church-related colleges and a lower percentage of junior colleges than the country as a whole. The latter figure is raised, however, if one considers the fourteen extension centers of Indiana University and Purdue University as equivalent to junior colleges.

This paper, therefore, has drawn its conclusions, which we believe are relevant for all American undergraduate education, from an intensive study of the kind of education concerning the non-Western areas of the world which the colleges and universities of the state of Indiana now provide their undergraduates, of the problems these institu-

116

tions face with regard to this particular subject, and of the objectives, methods, and ideas of administrators and faculty. It is based on the firm conviction that liberal education is indispensable to American democracy and that a thorough knowledge of American and other Western history, institutions, and values must constitute the core of American liberal education. On the other hand, it also assumes that knowledge of other areas and cultures must be diffused throughout our educational system if the latter is to keep pace with the vast changes which now affect the world and our role in it.

The survey began with a careful study of the catalogs and other published information of the Indiana universities and colleges. Visits were then made to each campus and conversations were held with presidents, deans, faculty members, and librarians. Thirty-four institutions enrolling approximately 65,000 undergraduates were studied in this fashion (see pp. 155-56 for a list of the institutions). Of these, three large universities—Indiana, Notre Dame, and Purdue—and their extension centers account for approximately half the total. Two large teachers colleges—Indiana State, at Terre Haute, and Ball State, at Muncie—have a combined total of about 7,500 undergraduates. The remaining twenty-nine institutions have an average undergraduate enrollment of slightly less than 1,000, with a range of about 250 to 2,000. Of these twenty-nine colleges, twenty are small (under 1,000 in all but one case), church-related institutions: twelve Protestant and eight Catholic. Three are small technical and engineering colleges, five are predominantly nonsectarian liberal arts institutions (al-

117

though four of these have a nominal tie with a Protestant denomination), and one is a junior college. Twenty-five of the thirty-four institutions are accredited by the North Central Association of Colleges and Secondary Schools.

II

Situation in the State of Indiana. Twenty-eight of the thirty-four institutions of higher education in Indiana are generally classed as liberal arts colleges. In only six of these institutions, however, do the majority of the students follow a purely liberal arts program. In fourteen colleges, the majority of the students are enrolled in teacher training programs which include a number of education courses, or in semiprofessional curricula (technical, business administration, pre-seminary, nursing, etc.) which include a number of specialized technical courses not of a liberal arts nature. In eight schools, about half the students follow a liberal arts program, with the other half in teacher training or semiprofessional programs. On the basis of this survey, it is clear that a large number of potential teachers in American elementary and secondary schools are being trained outside of the teachers colleges and in what are generally considered liberal arts colleges. Therefore, an increase in the attention devoted to non-Western areas of the world in the undergraduate colleges would soon have a significant impact upon secondary and, to some extent, elementary education.

Teachers colleges themselves present a special opportunity so far as education relating to non-Western areas

118

is concerned. The two large teachers colleges in Indiana have more than 7,000 students each year, while the School of Education in Indiana University and the program in education at Purdue University reach several hundred more. Most of the students in these schools learn almost nothing concerning the non-Western world, and only one or two per cent study a foreign language for even two years. In large part, this situation is a result, as it is in most colleges, of heavy emphasis in the required curriculum on courses dealing with the history and traditions of American and Western civilization. In addition, students in the teachers colleges are generally required to allot about one-seventh of their total program to courses in educational techniques and in practice teaching. Consequently, they can take only a limited number of elective courses, few of which, in any case, deal with non-Western problems. Nevertheless, these students as teachers, particularly as social studies teachers in American history, world history, and problems-of-democracy courses, are expected to help educate their students concerning areas and problems in the world about which their own information is at best rudimentary.

According to the testimony of teachers-college faculty members, a number of teachers in training are interested in learning about the non-Western world and in preparing themselves to carry some knowledge of other cultures to their students. The current trend in teacher education toward requiring a fifth year of preparation for a number of teachers may afford real opportunities for the development and satisfaction of such interests. In general, it is clear

119

that primary and secondary education in Indiana would be enormously broadened and enriched in the long run if students in the teachers colleges and schools of education received greater incentive and opportunity to acquire some knowledge of the non-Western areas.

While teachers colleges offer a special opportunity for education concerning non-Western areas, the technical institutions present a particular problem. As a rule, students in such schools complete substantially less work in the humanities and social sciences than do students in other institutions; consequently, they are normally even less exposed to material concerning the non-Western world. The liberal arts courses in these schools are therefore especially important, not only for the student as a citizen but notably for the growing number of technicians in fields such as agriculture and petroleum engineering who may eventually engage in overseas work for private companies, the federal government, or international organizations.

On the other hand, Soviet scientific and technical achievements have raised the question of instruction in the Russian language to some prominence in the technical institutions. Several administrators and faculty members in these schools believe that Russian language training should be made available for undergraduates in science and engineering, particularly for those who may go on to graduate study. Purdue University offers Russian, which is taken by over one hundred students. Rose Polytechnic Institute has recently appointed a language instructor to teach German; his major language competence is Russian, however,, and he may offer Russian in the near future.

The Curriculum. Generally, and properly, Indiana undergraduate curricula are oriented strongly toward the history, tradition, and thought of Western European and American civilization. At the same time, scant attention is paid to the non-Western cultures. For example, at even such an outstanding small college as Earlham, with its long tradition of interest in foreign areas, only 4.2 per cent of the total student semester hours in 1957-58 were in courses having some non-Western content, and only 14 per cent in courses, excluding languages, having substantial international and foreign content of all kinds (West European, Latin-American, and non-Western).[2]

In the Indiana colleges and universities as a whole, the introductory courses taken in the social sciences and humanities by the majority of undergraduate students (some undergraduates have no courses in the social sciences or humanities) refer to Russia, East Central Europe, and Asia only in passing, and to Africa hardly at all. Even the eleven courses which are histories of world civilization or general introductions to world civilization (see Table II-1) treat non-Western cultures briefly and focus primarily on Western civilization. Most instructors in these courses have concentrated on the United States or Western Europe in their graduate study; consequently, they tend to give most attention to the subject matter they know best. Nevertheless, the "world civilization" courses include more non-Western history than do the surveys of European civiliza-

2. These statistics were compiled by Professor Joseph D. Coppock, of Earlham College, for a discussion paper presented to the conference at Indiana University in September, 1958.

TABLE II-1. INDIANA INSTITUTIONS OFFERING BASIC GENERAL COURSES
WHICH TOUCH BRIEFLY ON NON-WESTERN AREAS, 1957-1958

Course	Number of Institutions	Per Cent of Total
World civilization	11	32
History of European civilization	20	59
World literature	25	74
Geography	24	70
Economics	3	9
Fine arts	12	35

tion, which are the basic courses in history in most institutions.

In the humanities, twenty-five institutions offer a course on world literature; such a course is generally required for those in training to teach elementary school. Here again, however, the attention given non-Western cultures is minimal. In most cases, students read six or eight brief selections from Asian writers; *Crime and Punishment*, by Dostoievsky, or a Tolstoy novel; and a play or short story by Chekhov. Generally, this is the only attention devoted to non-Western areas in humanities courses, except where a course on comparative religions or an advanced course on modern drama or literature is offered. Such courses nod at least in the direction of other areas and cultures as they rush along. Even so, the advanced literature or drama courses, while usually including a few Russian novels or plays, seldom mention an Asian author, and never an African one.

A few other general courses in particular disciplines devote some degree of attention to the non-Western world. For example, although there is considerable variation

122

TABLE II-2. INDIANA INSTITUTIONS OFFERING ADVANCED OR SPECIALIZED
COURSES WHICH DEAL IN PART WITH NON-WESTERN AREAS, 1957-1958

Course[a]	Number of Institutions	Per Cent of Total
Europe in the Twentieth Century	18	53
American Diplomatic History	17	50
European Diplomatic History	2	6
Comparative Government	15	44
International Relations	16	47
Current Events	4	12
Political, Social, or Economic Thought	18	53
Comparative Economic Systems	8	24
Economics of Underdeveloped Countries	3	9
Sociology or Cultural Anthropology	12	35
Philosophy (History of, or Contemporary)	24	70
Comparative Religions	17	50
Foreign Missions	8	24

[a] In most cases, these are one-semester courses given in alternate years and enroll primarily juniors and seniors, predominantly majors in the given discipline.

in the way geographers treat non-Western areas and materials, some introductory geography courses—variously called "world geography," "regional geography," "economic geography," etc.—touch briefly on the non-Western parts of the world, as do surveys of European history. The latter generally deal cursorily with the rise of Russia, the expansion of Europe overseas, Marxism, imperialism and colonialism, the rise of nationalism in East Central Europe, and the events of the twentieth century, in which Russia and Asia play an important role. In economics, only one or two of the beginning principles-of-economics courses give more than a passing glance to noncapitalist or non-Western economic systems. Occasionally, general courses

123

in art and music present a smattering of Oriental art and music or of Orthodox Church music. As a rule, the introductory or basic courses in the other disciplines ignore non-Western areas.

Almost every institution in Indiana offers at least a few advanced and specialized courses which treat non-Western developments more extensively than do the basic courses (see Table II-2). These, however, as well as those very few courses which deal specifically with a non-Western area, are all advanced courses taken by a relatively small number of junior and senior students, usually majors in the given discipline. Moreover, such courses are generally offered only in alternate years. As a result, only a small proportion of the student body is exposed to non-Western areas even in institutions which offer courses relating to these areas.

In history, courses in American diplomatic history, European diplomatic history, and Europe in the twentieth century (all generally for one semester) devote considerably more attention to the non-Western world than do the survey courses in the history of world civilization or of European civilization. Nevertheless, the main emphasis is upon Western Europe or the United States, and world problems are considered from the point of view of the United States or Western Europe.

Only eight institutions offer courses in comparative economic systems. These are all one-semester courses, and they generally follow a standard division, comparing the free enterprise, mixed, state capitalistic (Fascist), and Communist economic systems. Only three institutions (two of them major universities) offer courses which deal directly and in some detail with the economics of underdeveloped countries; and these courses seldom attract more than ten students.

In political science (sometimes called politics or government), several types of courses—comparative government, international relations, and political theory—deal in part with non-Western areas and materials. The comparative government courses generally devote approximately equal amounts of time to democratic, Fascist, and Communist types of government. These courses give little, if any, attention to Asian political institutions.

The courses on international relations or world politics customarily spend much time and effort on the principles of international relations, international organization, and international law. In dealing with current or recent developments, however, they naturally accord some attention to the role of Russia, Asia, and Africa.

Courses in social, political, or economic thought, which are located in different departments in different institutions, but which frequently cover a range of theory, usually treat Marxism-Leninism only briefly, and often with little expertness. Asian thought is seldom mentioned. Courses on the history of philosophy or on modern or contemporary philosophy occasionally refer to Oriental philosophy or to Marxism-Leninism. Seventeen institutions, mainly Protestant church-related schools, offer courses in comparative religions, which usually touch on Hinduism, Islam, Buddhism, and Confucianism. Similarly, eight church-related colleges offer courses on the history or philosophy

125

of foreign missions; these naturally deal to some extent with non-Western areas, particularly the Far East and Africa.

In sociology and cultural anthropology, several institutions offer courses, under various names, which examine race, population, or cross-cultural problems. These sometimes draw upon non-Western areas and experience, although they usually concentrate upon American problems.

Twenty institutions in Indiana offer one or more courses dealing specifically with a non-Western area or language. However, except for Indiana University and the University of Notre Dame, which have graduate programs in non-Western areas, only five institutions—Ball State Teachers College, DePauw University, Earlham College, Purdue University, and Valparaiso University—offer more than three courses which deal mainly with a non-Western area or language. On the other hand, half a dozen or more institutions are actively considering adding at least one more course on a non-Western area within the next two years, and eight intend to add instruction in the Russian language. Of those foreign-area courses offered, only three or four are taught by men who have received special training on the area; the others are given by instructors who have not had specialized training, although they are often much interested, and have frequently done a remarkably effective job of educating themselves for teaching on the area.

The great bulk of the area courses are concerned with Russia or the Far East; only four courses deal with Africa and two with the Middle East. East Central Europe receives practically no attention, except at Indiana University and

126

the University of Notre Dame, and in an incidental fashion in Russian history courses. The special courses devoted to non-Western areas are overwhelmingly in history (see Table II-3). Eight institutions offer Russian history every year, with an estimated three hundred students enrolled in these courses during 1957-58. Five colleges give Russian history in alternate years, generally for only a semester,

TABLE II-3. INDIANA INSTITUTIONS OFFERING SPECIAL COURSES
ON NON-WESTERN AREAS, 1957-1958

Course	Annually	Alternate Years	Total	Per Cent of Total Institutions	Number of Institutions Interested in Offering Courses
Far Eastern History[a]	5	11	16	47	2
Russian History[a]	8	5	13[b]	38	4
Asian Geography	2	3	5	15	...
Russian Geography	2	2	4	12	...
African Geography	1	2	3	9	...
History of Middle East	...	2	2	6	...
Introduction to Asia and the U.S.S.R.	...	1	1	3	...
Introduction to Africa	...	1	1	3	...
Russian Language	8[c]		8[d]	24	8
Uralic and Turkic Languages	1	...	1	3	...
Chinese Language	1	...	1	3	...

[a] In two institutions, these courses are two semesters in length; otherwise, they are one-semester courses.

[b] Another college added Russian history in the fall of 1958.

[c] These courses are noncredit courses in three institutions.

[d] In addition, two more colleges planned to introduce Russian language instruction in the fall of 1958.

127

with an average total enrollment of approximately eighty when the courses are offered. Thus, of the total Indiana undergraduate population of approximately 65,000, only about 1,360 students, or two per cent, study the history of Russia in any four-year period. In view of the importance of Russia in the lives of all of us, this is an alarming situation. One hopeful sign is that another college introduced Russian history in the fall of 1958, and four others hope to add such a course in the near future.

Five institutions offer a course in Far Eastern history every year, with a total enrollment of about 180 students. Eleven colleges present Far Eastern history in alternate years; approximately 185 students are enrolled in these courses when they are offered. Consequently, over four years, only about 1,100 Indiana undergraduates, or under 2 per cent, study Far Eastern history. All but two of the courses in Far Eastern history are one semester in length. About half of them comprise a brief historical survey of China and Japan, usually with some incidental attention to India; the remainder concentrate upon the modern history and politics of China, Japan, and, to some extent, India. Two institutions are anxious to introduce Far Eastern history courses.

Indiana institutions offer only a few other courses which deal specifically with non-Western areas. There are two courses on Middle Eastern history and institutions (both customarily taught by natives of the area), five courses on the geography of Asia, four on Russian geography, and three on African geography. One college offers in alternate years either an introduction to Asia and the Soviet Union or an introduction to Africa, courses which touch on geography, history, politics, and culture.

Only one Indiana institution, Indiana University, has offered an undergraduate major or minor in a non-Western area, and it has wisely abandoned its undergraduate majors in both the Russian and the East Central European fields on the grounds that too intensive specialization on an area at the undergraduate level often detracts from the broad preparation in the social sciences, humanities, and sciences which should be the principal objective of a liberal arts education. Indeed, we found no interest in undergraduate area majors in any institution in the state. At the same time, and regrettably, no institution in Indiana—probably only a few in the entire country—requires its undergraduates to pass a course dealing specifically with a foreign area, except for foreign language courses, when they are required.

Twenty-five of the colleges surveyed require two years of a foreign language for the B. A. degree. This statistic is somewhat misleading, however, as an indicator of the number of Indiana undergraduates studying foreign languages, since the foreign language requirement applies only to those students in a liberal arts program. Those preparing for teaching, even in a B. A. program, are generally not required to study a foreign language, and those taking a pre-professional program or working toward a B. S. degree (education, business administration, etc.) also miss this opportunity to obtain insight into a foreign culture. Moreover, students in almost all institutions are allowed to count high-school foreign language study as one year of credit toward the foreign language requirement. Consequently, less than half the Indiana undergraduates do in fact study any modern foreign language.

It is hardly surprising, therefore, that very little training in non-Western languages is offered in Indiana colleges and universities. Only eight of the thirty-four institutions in the state offer courses in the Russian language, and three of these institutions offer the course on a noncredit basis. Other non-Western languages are available to undergraduates only at Indiana University, which offers courses in Uralic, Turkic, Chinese, and a number of East Central European languages.

While it seems unlikely that the smaller colleges will be able to offer Asian, East Central European, or African languages in the near future, there is considerable interest in introducing the Russian language soon. Two colleges and three Indiana University extension centers began Russian language instruction in the fall of 1958, three other institutions hope to offer Russian by the fall of 1959, and five other institutions expressed a concrete interest in adding Russian in the near future. In most cases, the problem of obtaining teachers qualified to give Russian language courses is a serious one.

In assessing the possibilities for the expansion of Russian language instruction in the Indiana colleges, two factors deserve consideration. One is mounting student and faculty interest in Russian; the other, the belief of some administrators and instructors that Russian lacks the utility and the cultural significance of Western European languages. Several institutions reported definite expressions of student demand for Russian. These have sometimes taken the form of indirect requests channeled through modern-language teachers or faculty members interested in Russian affairs; in several cases, undergraduates have attempted to start informal faculty-student groups for noncredit study of Russian; in one instance, ten students submitted to their dean a formal petition for the introduction of a Russian language course. In colleges in which a significant number of undergraduates plan graduate study, this student interest will undoubtedly be an increasingly important factor in deciding whether to introduce Russian, particularly as more graduate schools recommend Russian as a second language for the doctoral degree.

Extracurricular Activity. At a number of institutions, extracurricular activities of various sorts constitute one of the most important and effective ways of exposing students to non-Western cultures. The most common approach is through the chapel meeting, lecture series, or assembly, at which speakers from the institution, outside lecturers, concerts, and films are presented. More than three-quarters of the Indiana colleges and universities have sponsored speakers on some aspect of world affairs within the last two years. A dozen of these institutions have arranged at least one meeting which dealt primarily with a non-Western society. In addition, eight institutions have offered film series containing one or more travelogues, documentaries, or commercial movies dealing with a non-Western area.

Sometimes such extracurricular activity is carefully coordinated with course work; this multiplies the impact and increases student interest. In some colleges, appropriate classes discuss and review the program. Occasionally, out-

131

side speakers meet with classes or hold informal faculty-student seminars or discussion groups.

The assembly type of extracurricular activity has the advantage of reaching a large majority of the student body. Moreover, lectures, concerts, and films frequently are open to the public and attract interested persons from the community. At the same time, they are incidental and passing events, a quick injection of information and interest, which, whatever the short-run benefits, may have little lasting influence. Few institutions enable a zealous student to build upon such an introduction to the non-Western world in his course work or in other extracurricular activity.

Another approach, but semicurricular in nature and with a longer and more intensive impact, is the presence for a year, a semester, or even a few weeks of a visiting professor or lecturer who is a specialist on a non-Western area. In addition to public lectures, such individuals may give special courses or seminars for students and faculty or may participate in established courses and seminars. Within the last few years, only a few Indiana institutions have benefited from this type of activity, probably because it is expensive and difficult to arrange. Several years ago Wabash was host to a visiting professor of Chinese philosophy and civilization. Indiana University annually receives visits of two weeks' duration from several members of the American Universities Field Staff, highly trained specialists who engage in study and research abroad for considerable periods of time. These men return to the United States every eighteen months to visit the universities cooperating

132

in the AUFS program, where they give lectures and participate in courses and seminars, drawing upon their knowledge and recent experience in the area of their special interest.

A related extracurricular technique is that of the special faculty or student group, assisted by outside participants. This sometimes takes the form of a faculty seminar meeting throughout the academic year on a particular curricular or substantive problem. In one especially effective case, two neighboring institutions developed a summer workshop for their faculty members. Such activities have been encouraged by the Lilly Foundation and by the Faculty Workshop program of the North Central Association of Colleges and Secondary Schools. In the latter program, a faculty member, after a summer of intensive study of a particular problem, conducts a faculty seminar during the following academic year.

One institution sponsored a series of "economic dinners" over a six-week period, open to students, faculty, and interested members of the community. Under this program, which was successful in every way, a panel of four economists from other institutions lectured and led a discussion one night each week. Other schools have tried brief special institutes or seminars on particular problems, with excellent results.

The most common type of extracurricular activity undertaken on student initiative is that connected with international relations clubs or similar organizations. Such groups are active in a majority of the Indiana colleges. In most cases, the clubs sponsor student and faculty forums, panels, and social meetings. Outside speakers are occasionally invited, and special international programs, such as the convocation of a model UN Assembly for high school students from the surrounding area, are arranged. Inevitably, some students who belong to international relations clubs are interested, or become interested, in non-Western areas.

Most Indiana colleges have a small number of foreign students, many of them from the non-Western world, and the larger universities each have several hundred. These students reportedly have a greater impact upon the community than upon the student body itself. Foreign students are in considerable demand as speakers and guests at Rotary luncheons and club meetings, and many of them evidently represent their countries very effectively. Within the colleges, though, the foreign students appear to be taken somewhat for granted, and, with the exception of occasional close individual friendships with Americans or the sporadic arousing of student curiosity, they do not affect the outlook of the majority of undergraduates. At the same time, foreign students are often active in student groups and clubs, especially international relations clubs, and sometimes they organize cultural programs, dinners, international exhibits or fairs, and other special events at appropriate college ceremonies.

Ten Indiana institutions participate in radio-television programming in their communities. In most cases, several of the programs during the year relate to world affairs in some fashion, generally in the form of a panel discussion arranged by a class in the social sciences or by the inter-

134

national relations club, with both American and foreign students participating. These programs, which occasionally deal with the non-Western world, seem to meet with a favorable response, and there is probably considerable unexploited potential in this type of activity, both for arousing student interest in non-Western areas and for informing a segment of the public.

Teaching Materials and the Library. Teaching materials for instruction concerning non-Western areas are a major problem. Libraries and instructors need textbooks, written for the *undergraduate*, which put non-Western areas into greater prominence and better perspective, source materials and readings in inexpensive formats, and journals on non-Western areas of a less scholarly and more popular nature than most current ones. Many instructors now rely upon current newspapers, periodicals, and pamphlets for illustrative and supplementary material, particularly concerning recent or contemporary developments. Few make adequate use of films and television as teaching aids.

Most libraries (excluding those in the large universities) have almost no non-Western language materials, very few books in Western foreign languages on the non-Western areas, and only a few periodicals which deal with these areas. Moreover, their holdings in English on non-Western areas are limited and uneven; coverage of areas and subjects is spotty; and the materials vary widely in quality. Most libraries subscribe to one or two journals on international politics and world affairs, such as *Foreign Affairs* and *World Politics*, and to one or two distinguished newspapers. Outside of the large university libraries, only a few possess such journals as the *Far Eastern Survey* and *Problems of Communism;* one or two carry the *Middle East Journal* and the English language magazine issued by the Soviet government, *USSR;* only three subscribe to the *Current Digest of the Soviet Press,* an invaluable teaching aid for undergraduate courses touching on recent and contemporary Soviet affairs. Only three or four libraries purchase scholarly journals, such as the *American Slavic and East European Review,* and the *Journal of Asian Studies.*

III

The principal achievements with regard to education concerning the non-Western areas are, by nature, difficult to define because they reside in the spirit of education and in the atmosphere of the campus. Fundamentally, during the last decade or two, the horizons of Indiana colleges and of their students have stretched. While much remains to be done, given the magnitude of the problem and the conservative character of educational institutions, considerable progress has been made in adding new courses, in introducing new languages and techniques of language instruction, in injecting into the curricula and into the climate of education a new approach toward the rest of the world, in utilizing extracurricular methods effectively, and in absorbing into the college community men and women from other parts of the world.

Some institutions have inevitably progressed more than others. The two largest universities with a liberal arts foundation, Indiana and Notre Dame, have developed impressive graduate programs on non-Western areas. However, undergraduate instruction in both of these institutions has, thus far, been remarkably little affected by these additions, and these universities must erect a bridge from their graduate programs and research to the undergraduate student body. Purdue University in the last decade has expanded foreign language instruction and has enlarged the impact of the social sciences and humanities upon its technical studies. A number of the smaller institutions have become much concerned with the problem of exposing the undergraduate to the non-Western world and are developing promising new approaches to this problem. Earlham College, for example, is in the process of working out with Antioch College a cooperative arrangement for a basic course on the Far East as a means of acquainting its students with at least one major non-Western area. This basic course will, it is hoped, be included among those courses meeting the distribution requirement in the social sciences so that it may become a part of the educational experience of a substantial number of Earlham undergraduates. In addition, each college will offer one advanced course to permit interested students to learn about the area in somewhat greater depth.

Most Indiana administrators and instructors agree that undergraduates need to know more concerning non-Western civilizations. Sixteen, or approximately half, of the Indiana colleges have demonstrated sufficient interest in improving their curricula regarding the non-Western areas to seek to add instructors and courses. Nine colleges have a mild though definite interest, but will obviously need outside encouragement. Seven are interested but passive, and leaders in but two institutions doubt that the study of non-Western areas is important or that they should increase their efforts in this regard.

Present interest in non-Western areas on the part of Indiana colleges and universities is focused on the Far East and Russia, with little in South Asia and the Middle East, and almost none concerning Southeast Asia, Africa, and East Central Europe, except as the latter is considered a part of the Soviet orbit. Moreover, interest in Russia is increasing at a more rapid rate than that in other areas, undoubtedly because of the events of the last year or two, particularly the launching of the Soviet satellites. More institutions are planning the addition of Russian language instruction and Russian history courses than are planning courses in other area fields.

In those institutions with clear interests or considerable achievements in instruction concerning non-Western areas, one or two members of the faculty or administration are usually responsible. Such men are generally leaders within their institutions, and they clearly represent one of the most important resources for improving undergraduate instruction on the non-Western world. They are more significant than funds, materials, or special programs. They provide the indispensable initiative and leadership; they need only assistance and support.

Most colleges have been distressingly slow in bringing the fruits of modern technology into the educational process. Many are working with nineteenth-century practices and

138

equipment, and few make effective use of new methods and techniques, from audio-visual materials and devices to television. The new generation of teachers is generally not being trained to use modern aids in the classroom. Only three institutions in the state have modern-language laboratories, and only two others have even makeshift or experimental laboratories. Indiana libraries often ignore large parts of the world, and the undergraduate in many Indiana institutions would not be able to find one readable and informative book on some areas of the world, if he were interested.

Moreover, the various institutions in the state have not fully utilized available opportunities for a cooperative attack on the new problems which face them. Faculty members competent on non-Western areas or languages might be shared by neighboring institutions; other cooperative arrangements also seem to promise mutual benefits. Yet joint appointments seldom exist, even when institutions are only a few blocks or miles apart. Only rarely are visiting lecturers shared, and an experience in one institution is infrequently passed on to another.

In general, Indiana colleges and universities, as all institutions of higher learning in America, have been scrambling desperately, but often unsuccessfully, to have the education and inspiration they impart somehow reflect the changes which affect the world in this most revolutionary of ages. Most administrators recognize the problems; most realize that education must preserve the best, teach about our own society, and create a synthesis of the past and the present, of the old and the new. Few, however, have acted with the

139

deliberate speed necessary to prepare our students for life in the second half of the twentieth century. So far as non-Western areas are concerned, this is especially true of the technical and professional schools or curricula in all the Indiana institutions. In other words, most institutions must make an immense organized effort to meet this revolutionary challenge, or provide an education unworthy of their students and the times.

IV

What Can Be Done. Such is the situation in undergraduate education in Indiana. To those who are concerned over how well our youth are being prepared for responsible citizenship in the world of 1980—a world in which Russia, China, and all of Asia and Africa will be playing prominent roles, with their actions daily affecting the vital interests of the United States—the picture is a disturbing one. It is clear that the average Indiana undergraduate today receives an education so highly oriented toward Western civilization that he emerges from college with little understanding of or interest in world affairs or other cultures. The boundaries of his knowledge and interest resemble those which Santayana defined as "respectability and Christendom." We believe that this is the case in other states as well: Indiana curricula are not notably different, Indiana instructors come from every state in the Union, the textbooks and other materials used are also used in other states, and the Indiana record on foreign language instruction, while below the national average, is not an unusual one.

If this situation is to be changed, what are the major problems to be overcome and what lines of action can be followed? Fundamental is the need to recast and reorient our whole educational effort, from kindergarten to Ph. D. In this spectrum, the undergraduate years are vital. Alumni, administrators, and faculty of American colleges must recognize that traditional educational requirements fall short of meeting the needs of the twentieth-century world, that knowledge of Western culture alone will not suffice for the citizen of tomorrow, and that liberal education must be universal in outlook, drawing on the values, experience and aspirations of all peoples and cultures. It is not far-fetched to imagine the day when the study of non-Western societies will be regarded not as something unusual and exotic, requiring special interests and extraordinary resources, but as part of the normal activity of the social science and humanities departments of every college and university in the country. The time may also come when some knowledge of non-Western peoples and civilizations will be accepted as part of the customary intellectual baggage which should accompany every American undergraduate as he leaves the campus.

Such a broad rethinking of our educational emphases is, of course, a difficult task. It will not be accomplished overnight. Moreover, as all involved in education understand, the nature of man, of academic man in particular, assumes as much significance in this problem as the subject and the material. Educational systems are among the most conservative structures in existence. This report was, therefore, prepared and written in the same combination of hope and

141

despair which led one college president to compare changing the curriculum to moving a cemetery.

There are good grounds for optimism, however. The objectives of an educational system mirror the values of the society of which it is a part. Today, Americans as a whole are more "world-minded" than they have ever been; the events of the last two decades have forced upon our consciousness the existence and importance of the non-Western world. Moreover, and most encouragingly, the attitudes and climate within educational institutions are changing rapidly. Students are eager to learn about areas and peoples which they sense will some day significantly affect their own interests. Faculty are inquisitive and are reaching out for new data and new ideas by which to test old assumptions based almost solely on Western experience. Most administrators are aware of the immense new challenges which have arisen at the very moment when practical issues of the most compelling kind face every educational institution. As President Robert F. Goheen, of Princeton University, pointed out in his annual report for 1958, American universities and colleges, after "some two and a half centuries of academic preoccupation with the Western world—to the neglect of the Orient, when not to its exclusion," must now learn "to educate our citizenry effectively as regards the non-European world, with all of its vast requirements and the telling influence it is likely to have in the future course of this century."

All our colleges live in a different climate from that of twenty years ago. Television, radio, newspapers, and magazines provide information and an atmosphere concerning the rest of the world completely unlike that of a generation ago, and institutions whose faculty members were distributed throughout the world by war and cold war have gradually changed character and outlook. This is reflected in the vigor and vitality of the interest expressed in non-Western areas and the eagerness with which individuals and groups actively seek to improve the quality of instruction in this regard. These factors are difficult to define and to measure, but they constitute the liveliest hope for the future.

But a change of attitude and outlook is not enough. A growing number of educators recognize the importance of acquainting undergraduates with the non-Western areas, but many of them believe that this objective has to be neglected, or at best given a low priority, until students know better their own history and culture. They are concerned that there is simply not enough time in four crowded undergraduate years to inform a student adequately concerning both the Western and non-Western worlds. Moreover, others, deeply interested in instruction regarding non-Western areas, are hampered by practical problems, particularly those of course and curriculum reorganization and those connected with finding and paying for additional faculty and library materials.

The remaining pages of this paper are therefore devoted to a discussion of various practical measures that may be taken to increase the attention devoted to non-Western cultures in an undergraduate institution. These suggestions are based on the ideas of the Indiana presidents, deans, and faculty interviewed and on the discussion of this problem

143

at the conference held at Indiana University in September, 1958. In most cases, the steps outlined here involve little, if any, reduction or dilution of education concerning the Western world, which has been the colleges' chief concern. These suggestions certainly do not exhaust the possibilities for action, but are those considered most useful and immediately feasible for most colleges. Moreover, they are, in most instances, procedures which can be adopted at once and at little cost. Clearly, not all these courses of action are applicable to every institution; each college will want to select those most suited to its needs.

In the first place, even with the best of intentions, it is difficult for administrators and faculty concerned with this problem to undertake to resolve it entirely on their own. Often, they are not informed concerning the experience of other institutions, from which they might profit. They do not know where to turn for guidance concerning puzzling questions connected with the curriculum and with the acquisition of books and teachers. Under these circumstances, it is clear that many educators would welcome and be helped by advice and assistance from area specialists and from other college teachers and administrators concerned with undergraduate education relating to non-Western areas. This assistance might come from a graduate area center or from groups of area specialists. For example, the survey revealed that Indiana colleges would welcome guidance and aid concerning instruction in non-Western areas from Indiana University or from an organization of specialists established for this purpose. Indeed, state or regional cen-

144

ters for each non-Western area could provide most useful guidance for those seeking to improve undergraduate education.

Over the next few years, the area specialists will undoubtedly develop specific mechanisms for the purpose of assisting and advising colleges interested in this question. In the field of Asian studies, the Asia Society, with headquarters in New York, already performs such functions, making available information on undergraduate programs of Asian studies, distributing lists of appropriate books and films, organizing traveling cultural and art exhibits, and helping to arrange consulting services on the problems involved in introducing Asian studies. In the interim, any college which wishes to secure help and guidance for improving the position of non-Western studies in its curriculum will find a sympathetic response from area centers in neighboring universities.

Plans will also undoubtedly be devised to permit teachers and administrators interested in instruction concerning non-Western areas to meet with area specialists on a regional basis every few years. Such conferences could either concentrate on the problems and opportunities involved in courses on non-Western areas or might deal with substantive issues concerning given areas. These conferences would stimulate college teachers, educate specialists concerning the needs and the achievements of undergraduate instruction, and in general bridge the gap which separates the university and the college, the specialist and the teacher. Indeed, high school teachers should also participate in these conferences,

145

because the educational process is a continuum, and no one part can be repaired if all parts are not in good order and close cooperation.

The most urgent problem is to determine how to expose all, or practically all, undergraduates to the non-Western world in some form. When the question of enlarging the role of non-Western studies is raised, some educators think immediately of the addition of specialized courses on the history, government, economy, or literature of given areas. In fact, such advanced courses in particular disciplines, while representing an important complementary approach to the problem, are usually elected by only a few junior and senior students and consequently reach only a small proportion of the student body.

An essential step therefore is to increase the attention devoted to non-Western areas in basic general courses in the social sciences and humanities, which are required of a large number of students at the freshman and sophomore level. These are sometimes called "general education" courses and usually bear disciplinary designations, such as world history, introductory geography, world literature, or principles of economics. This increase in attention may be achieved by some reorganization of course content or by the introduction of comparative and illustrative material from non-Western areas. Recasting such basic courses can be encouraged by providing a faculty member with free time, perhaps with outside financial support, to revise a given course, to develop a new syllabus and readings, and to prepare necessary new materials pertaining to non-Western areas.

146

An alternative approach is the development of an inter-departmental introductory or civilization course on a non-Western culture, such as the one on the Far East being planned at Earlham and Antioch, to match the traditional course devoted to a survey of European history or Western civilization. It is essential that such a course occupy a position in the curriculum or the college requirements that will ensure enrollment of a majority of the freshman or sophomore students. The planning and introduction of this type of course inevitably involve substantial problems relating to personnel, materials, departmental organization, and finances, but, here again, advice and assistance from those with experience in these matters would be most helpful.

Steps to increase the non-Western content of undergraduate education can also be taken at the upper division or junior and senior level. More non-Western materials can be introduced into existing comparative courses, such as, comparative government, comparative economic systems, international relations, and comparative religion, or such courses can be initiated. Finally, some institutions may find it possible to introduce special disciplinary courses devoted to parts of the non-Western world, such as the geography of Asia, Russian history, or Soviet economic development.

It seems unlikely that the average college will be able to offer instruction in the languages of Asia and Africa in the immediate future. Opportunities for interested undergraduates to study these languages will undoubtedly be made available through summer programs at major university area and language centers, particularly with the assist-

147

ance provided under Title VI of the National Defense Education Act of 1958, which is specifically designed to promote American knowledge of the "unusual" languages.

However, a number of colleges should be in a position to offer Russian language instruction in the course of the next decade. Russian is easier to teach and to learn than most Asian and African languages, and it is rapidly rivaling German and French in importance as a language of science. Knowledge of Russian permits direct access to the great literary and cultural heritage of Russian civilization and also has utilitarian value for the growing number of Americans who have contact with the Soviet world—government officials, scholars, journalists, artists, students, and ordinary tourists. Many graduate schools now accept Russian as one of the languages meeting requirements for a doctoral degree, and some science departments strongly recommend Russian for graduate work. In the teaching of Russian, modern methods of language instruction should be employed, and a minimum of two years of course work should be offered. Students should be encouraged to begin the study of Russian and other European languages as early as possible in their educational careers.

Adding interested and qualified teachers is a major hurdle in the development of non-Western studies in undergraduate education. However, the expected mushrooming of student enrollment should provide a unique opportunity for the addition of area-trained teachers to college staffs. In the normal replacement and expansion of faculty, colleges will be able to appoint good teachers with a double competence: sound training in a discipline combined with area specialization or, in the case of language teachers, German or French, as well as Russian. Such individuals can carry their share of teaching in the basic disciplinary courses or in the customary languages, while at the same time broadening and enriching the curriculum through their knowledge of a particular non-Western area or language. It is admittedly difficult at present for the college administrator to identify and attract teachers with this sort of dual capability. Once again, however, an organization providing guidance and help concerning instruction on the non-Western areas, or the area centers themselves, could be of assistance.

At the same time, the universities must to some degree recast graduate education. In many cases, graduate schools are still producing students oriented almost exclusively toward Western institutions and culture, or specialists so highly trained on non-Western areas that they cannot teach a basic disciplinary course effectively. A heavy share of the responsibility for encouraging greater attention to non-Western areas in undergraduate education lies with the graduate schools and their respective discipline departments, which must provide a different kind of product, particularly men and women with strong training in their discipline and sound knowledge concerning at least one non-Western area.

The major universities and their specialists can contribute substantially to progress in undergraduate education in still another way: by recognizing the shortage of teaching materials and by changing their values for prestige and promotion. Thus, senior scholars should be encouraged to

149

write textbooks for basic general courses in the disciplines which devote increased attention to the non-Western world and to prepare and publish texts and other teaching materials on individual areas. This would be of enormous assistance to the undergraduate teacher, handicapped now by the shortage or absence of such materials.

In meeting the need for teachers prepared to instruct concerning non-Western areas in the colleges, existing faculty resources, as well as new appointments, can be utilized. A number of undergraduate institutions have teachers keenly interested in presenting courses dealing with non-Western areas or languages. A fellowship program to enable such teachers to obtain additional training on the area or its languages at a major university center, for a period ranging from one or two summers to fifteen months, would constitute an important step in expanding faculty resources on the non-Western areas. At the center, the instructor would audit and observe courses, collect reading lists, attend seminars, discuss instructional problems with specialists and other teachers, and obtain knowledge and stimulation for his own teaching. Such a program would be easy to arrange for a summer, and members of several departments at Indiana University are already planning summer school programs especially designed for this purpose and for "refreshing" instructors who received training and experience in non-Western areas some years ago. In 1958-59, the Center for East Asian Studies at Harvard University inaugurated a fellowship program under which liberal arts colleges and the Center cooperate in providing a year's study at Harvard to teachers of undergraduate courses interested in improving instruction concerning the East Asian area in their institutions.

While arrangements to release a teacher for additional training in a non-Western area have to be worked out carefully between the college and the sponsoring center, there are no insurmountable obstacles. Many institutions are willing to share the expenses involved, although in most cases fellowship aid would probably also be required. In some instances, faculty members might take advantage of sabbatical and other established leave arrangements. In the Indiana colleges alone, a half a dozen or more able and interested candidates for such a program were found, surely a fine sign for the future. As noted previously, another group of teachers could effectively use leave, probably on their own campuses, to revise their basic courses and to add new materials concerning non-Western areas to established general courses. Faculty travel and faculty exchanges, sometimes privately sponsored, sometimes under government auspices, represent still another significant avenue for extending teaching resources on the non-Western areas.

Finally, cooperative arrangements among neighboring institutions are an important way to multiply the offerings and capabilities of colleges interested in non-Western studies. Such arrangements hold particular promise in the language field. In cases where two institutions are very close, students of one might take classes at the other college, or faculty might be shared. Another possibility to be fully explored is beaming TV courses on non-Western areas from one institution to a number of institutions, a program which Indiana University launched with several colleges in

151

the spring of 1959 with a course on modern Russian history. Cooperation among faculty members and in courses of the kind being contemplated by Earlham and Antioch should be considered. Moreover, in expanding their work on non-Western areas, colleges should always endeavor to complement rather than duplicate the resources of neighboring institutions. Cooperative efforts of all kinds can, of course, embrace library materials, as well as courses and faculty.

The realm of extracurricular and semicurricular activity offers a wide range of possibilities. Special efforts can ensure increased attention to the non-Western world in chapel and assembly programs, in lecture and film series, in panels and forums, in debates, in the work of international relations clubs and similar groups, in exhibits and festivals, and in radio-TV programming sponsored by the college. A number of opportunities exist for enlisting the interest and cooperation of groups in the community. In addition, assistance and advice can often be obtained from such national organizations in the foreign affairs field as the Foreign Policy Association, the Council on Foreign Relations, and regional Councils on World Affairs. The role of the foreign student in the college community can be made more meaningful. Student travel and exchanges have always represented an excellent method of interesting and informing undergraduates concerning the non-Western world.

Finally, there is great potential in the development, through cooperation between the colleges and the area centers, of a system of visiting seminars or workshops, bringing individual specialists or groups of area specialists to a campus for intensive discussion of an area with both faculty and students. These specialists might be distinguished scholars; they might also be lively young students, still in graduate school or just beginning their careers, who have completed a period of study in their area of special concern and who can bring the particular insights of young men and women to undergraduate student bodies. Such a program might consist of six or eight weekly meetings or a continuous three-day session; it would involve community participation, visits to appropriate classes, meetings with interested groups, and seminars or discussions with faculty members. While the effect of such brief "institutes" might not be lasting, the immediate impact on both the college and the community would undoubtedly be significant, and the long-range result would almost certainly be much increased faculty and student effort and interest concerning the study of non-Western areas.

As noted earlier in the report, there is an urgent need for textbooks and other materials for the undergraduate which give sufficient attention to the non-Western world, a need which can be adequately met only if the academic profession and university administrators begin to recognize the importance of, and give due credit for, the preparation of such materials by competent scholars in the various area fields. At the same time, publishers can do much to assist by encouraging and supporting the writing of textbooks and the compiling of source books which contain substantial material on the non-Western world.

In the library field, a most important and immediately useful step would be the preparation of a critical bibliogra-

153

phy on the non-Western areas, providing the kind of information an instructor or librarian needs to help him identify the significant books. An area specialist, or a committee of area specialists, in whose judgment the colleges would have confidence, might select and evaluate lists of books and periodicals on non-Western areas. Two types of lists are needed: one, issued once but revised periodically, would describe a basic collection for each area; the other, issued annually, would analyze the most important works on each area published within the preceding year. The former list would permit a library to check its present holdings and to begin an acquisition program designed to obtain the most fundamental and useful books on the non-Western areas. The latter would assist a library in continuing to build a first-rate small collection and in wisely expending its monies for current acquisitions.

Finally, the potential of various audio-visual and other technical aids remains to be fully exploited. Instruction concerning the non-Western areas would benefit greatly from improved materials of this sort and from a greater realization on the part of teachers of the utility and value of such teaching aids.

In conclusion, we should like to emphasize our conviction, buttressed by achievements in a number of institutions, that very considerable progress in instruction concerning the non-Western areas can be made by any college at little cost. Because the problem is such an important and seemingly formidable one, some college educators may assume that its resolution is beyond their reach. In fact, however, any college can make a start, drawing upon the suggestions advanced in this paper and on others which are bound to occur to alert faculty and administrators. A major change, even a revolution, in an institution's approach to this problem can be attained in a number of ways, many of which involve little expense or dislocation. With interest and determination, American students can be made aware of the problems and potentialities of the non-Western world and be prepared to live in the age which lies ahead.

APPENDIX: THE COLLEGES AND UNIVERSITIES OF INDIANA

Anderson College (Church of God)
Ball State Teachers College
Butler University (Disciples of Christ association)
Concordia Senior College (Lutheran—Missouri Synod)
DePauw University (Methodist association)
Earlham College (Society of Friends)
Evansville College (Methodist association)
Franklin College (Baptist)
Goshen College (Mennonite)
Grace Theological Seminary and College (Grace Brethren)
Hanover College (Presbyterian association)
Huntington College (Church of United Brethren)
Indiana Central College (Evangelical United Brethren)
Indiana State Teachers College
Indiana Technical College
Indiana University
  Indiana University Extension Centers

155

Calumet—East Chicago
Evansville (with Evansville College)
Fort Wayne
Gary
Indianapolis
Jeffersonville—New Albany
Kokomo
Richmond (with Earlham College)
South Bend—Mishawaka
Vincennes (with Vincennes University)
Manchester College (Church of Brethren)
Marian College (Catholic)
Marion College (Wesleyan Methodist)
Oakland City College (Baptist)
Purdue University
  Purdue University Extension Centers
    Columbus
    Fort Wayne
    Hammond
    Indianapolis
    Michigan City
Rose Polytechnic Institute
St. Francis College (Catholic)
St. Joseph's College (Catholic)
St. Mary-of-the-Woods College (Catholic)
St. Mary's College (Catholic)
St. Meinrad's Seminary (Catholic)
Taylor University (Methodist association)
Tri-State College
University of Notre Dame (Catholic)

Valparaiso University (Lutheran)
Vincennes University (junior college)
Wabash College
West Baden College (Catholic)

3

The Study of Russia in Secondary Education

GEORGE BARR CARSON, JR.

CONSIDERATION[1] of the role of Russian studies in secondary education illustrates rather forcefully the well-known estrangement between American academic specialists and the teaching of their subject in the schools. There is a significant and rapidly growing interest in Russia and the Communist orbit among educational leaders and organizations concerned with the secondary schools. Some efforts to introduce the study of Russia and of the Russian language are under way, but only in exceptional cases—Russian language instruction might require qualification of this generalization—are the recognized specialists in the field actively involved.

An examination of what is taught today in American secondary schools indicates that the amount of material on Russia and the Communist orbit generally available is not

1. This paper is based on a conference of leaders in secondary education and scholars and teachers in Russian studies held in Washington,

158

very extensive. Those familiar with the secondary-school program agree that the only part of the curriculum which is likely to include any significant content on Russia is that in the social studies. Social studies courses vary widely from state to state and from district to district within states, even where there is some centralization of standards by a state office of education. In general, however, probably more information on Russia appears than ever before.

The pattern of social studies requirements is in flux. The pre-1914 standard of a four-year secondary-school sequence in history, composed of ancient, medieval, modern, and American history, has long been discarded in the great majority of public schools. That abandoned sequence offered little or no material on Russia except in the diplomatic history of modern Europe. The social studies courses

D. C., on October 17-19, 1958, under the joint sponsorship of the American Council of Learned Societies, the National Association of Secondary-School Principals, and the Joint Committee on Slavic Studies. It summarizes the findings of the conference, as well as the substance of its working papers, which have been published in the *Bulletin of the National Association of Secondary-School Principals*, XLIII (March, 1959), 117-215. At a second conference held in Washington, D. C., on May 28-29, 1959, under the joint sponsorship of the National Council for Social Studies, the National Association of Secondary-School Principals, and the American Council of Learned Societies, the needs of the secondary schools in materials and assistance were further discussed. These conferences and this paper are based on the conviction that secondary-school students need to know more not only about Russia but also about the other non-Western areas. Consequently, this consideration of the problem of devoting more attention to Russia in secondary education is viewed as a pilot study which, it is hoped, will also have pertinence for the development of the study of other non-Western areas in the secondary schools.

159

which supplanted the history sequence were intended to combine the approaches of a number of disciplines, but no appreciable change in the attention given to Eastern Europe marked the shift. Equally important, from the standpoint of introducing material on Russia in the schools today, the number of units in social studies required at varying times since the First World War has never equalled the four units of history cast out when the curriculum of the public secondary school ceased to center primarily around a college preparatory course and was transformed into universal general and vocational education.

In the present social studies program, all states require one unit (some form of American history and government). Many states require two units of social studies and some require three, but stipulate only one (American history and government) that is not open to individual election. A few schools may require four units of social studies; such a requirement is increasingly recommended for special programs for academically talented students, but specific courses are not stipulated. There are occasional exceptions, of course: Texas now has a state requirement that all secondary schools must give world history as well as American history.

Although the requirements vary, civics, world history, and world geography are generally offered in the ninth or tenth grades, and the first two are sometimes required. In the eleventh grade, American history is required. In the twelfth grade, problems of democracy, or a pair of semester courses (economics, government, sociology), or senior his-

160

tory, is sometimes required, but is usually elective. In addition to American history, required of all, approximately sixty per cent of secondary-school students take world history or some twelfth-grade variant of "problems." Available figures do not show whether the same forty per cent which fails to elect world history when it is not required also fails to elect "problems."

In so far as the secondary-school social studies program includes the study of Russia at all, such study generally forms part of the content of world history courses. In problems-of-democracy courses the problems taught vary, but they often include one on differing economic systems or one comparing the conditions of peoples who live under totalitarian and under democratic rule. In American history relatively little is studied about Russia, except in connection with World War I and World War II, and this is likely to be incidental. In civics, Russia is not likely to be studied other than as it appears for discussion in weekly current affairs. In world geography it may be studied, but relatively few pupils take this subject.

Immediately after World War II, Richard W. Burkhardt studied the question, "What is taught about the Soviet Union in American secondary schools?" through (1) a content analysis of social studies textbooks, (2) responses to a questionnaire sent to a sampling of teachers, and (3) the results of an information test on the Soviet Union given to sample groups of high school seniors.[2] Since few teachers

2. Richard W. Burkhardt, "The Teaching of the Soviet Union in American Secondary School Social Studies," doctoral dissertation, Graduate School of Education, Harvard University, 1950; and "Report

had had training in the language, literature, history, economics, or geography of Russia, study of Russia was
heavily dependent upon textbooks, Burkhardt concluded.
But students had little oportunity to learn about the Soviet
Union from their textbooks, which devoted little attention to this topic. Furthermore, some material that was included was misleading and inaccurate, and a major problem
was misplaced emphasis—too much attention to items of
relatively little importance concerning the U.S.S.R. and
inadequate presentation of significant material. Burkhardt's
analysis also suggested that full use was not being made of
the opportunities available for effective textbook presentation of the Soviet Union. An analysis of the textbooks
showed that much of the space given to less significant nations might have been used to present a more complete
picture of the Soviet Union.

Even in schools reported to have superior social studies
programs, students had little opportunity to study the
Soviet Union. Interested teachers reported dissatisfaction
with the presentation of Soviet affairs in textbooks and
described their need to rely on pamphlets and other current
materials to teach the most important information. Moreover, the little time devoted to study of the U.S.S.R. was
not being used as efficiently as it might have been because
there was no real agreement among teachers upon the most
vital topics to be taught. Students' knowledge of the Soviet
Union, reflecting their learning opportunities, showed that

on a Test of Information about the Soviet Union in American Secondary
Schools," *American Slavic and East European Review*, V (November,
1946), 1-28.

they did not know the really important data about the Soviet Union.

An examination of a small selection of textbooks, made in 1958 by Beth Arveson, of the University of Wisconsin High School, showed little significant change in the space allotted to Russia. On the whole, problems-of-democracy textbooks still give scant attention to Russia, although the world history textbooks usually have one or more chapters on Russia. Progress in this respect, over a period of ten to fifteen years, seems discouragingly slow, since it is clear that much the same comments about texts can be made today that were made by Burkhardt. But the more encouraging side of recent developments is the increase in supplementary materials available. These are being provided by teacher organizations, as, for example, the National Council for the Social Studies, through its yearbooks and its journal *Social Education*, and by state and federal educational agencies. The department of public instruction of the state of Pennsylvania published a guide to materials after making a study of the problem of teaching about Communism in the public schools.

If, as some students of public education assert, there is a thirty-year lag between introduction of a subject and its widespread acceptance, Russian studies in the secondary schools are following the traditional pattern. If, however, specialists in Russian studies exhibit a greater concern for the introduction of this subject in the schools, this will encourage and assist the growing number of teachers and administrators who have already shown interest and some initiative in this regard.

163

Significant exceptions to the pattern of introducing Russian studies through world history and problems-of-democracy courses occur. At the University of Wisconsin High School a substantial section on Russia was included in the senior social problems course beginning in February, 1958. While part of the inspiration for this initiative undoubtedly stemmed from the success of Russian satellite experiments a few months before, much of it was due to the general curiosity of the students about Russia and to the enthusiasm and long-term interest of their teacher. A full semester course on Russian history was introduced in the fall of 1958 at the same school. The program at the University of Wisconsin High School has the advantage of close collaboration between the teacher, Beth Arveson, who had not previously had special training in Russian studies, and a professor of Russian history at the university, Michael B. Petrovich. Other members of the university staff cooperate in special subjects, and for 1958-59 the Russian course in the high school is coordinated with television lectures by Professor Petrovich in a further experimental program.

Resources such as those at the University of Wisconsin are not available to most secondary schools. The classic pattern, however, for introduction of a new subject in the secondary-school curriculum is through the success of just such special experimental courses as those at the Wisconsin school. Multiplying examples of a similar sort would undoubtedly lead, in a period of ten or fifteen years, to the production of standardized teaching materials for the subject and to the gradual absorption of the material in some part of the social studies program. Whether courses relating to Russian studies in the secondary schools incorporate the information that Russian specialists in the several academic disciplines consider important may well depend upon their initiative in cooperating with social studies teachers in the organization of pilot courses and the preparation of materials which will set the pace for the majority of schools.

II

The great majority of secondary-school social studies teachers today have not had any training in Russian studies. Teacher preparation programs have been recurrently under pressure to make provision for the special interest of some particular group—among parents, educational psychologists, specialists in one or another academic discipline, and many others. The large number of special pressures, however, has had relatively little effect on the prevailing pattern of social studies courses in the curriculum. Since the education of teachers is closely related to the demands made by the established curriculum, the introduction of special training in a particular area is likely to be exceptional and dependent upon individual choice, or even chance, as much as upon design.

The secondary-school general education program in the social studies, as already indicated, is decidedly limited so far as Russian studies are concerned. Teacher education is correspondingly restricted. The question, then, as in the case of Russian studies in the secondary-school curriculum,

165

is where in the teacher preparation program the desirable training can be added, or how teachers already in service may acquire training in Russian studies.

Although the pattern of a five-year program for teacher preparation, and possibly a master's degree, is now often recognized as desirable, the four-year program is still generally in effect. Because of the multiple demands upon student time, specialization in a particular field, such as Russian studies, is difficult of achievement in the four-year program. Certain requirements in professional education must be met, while the general education must provide all of the substantive needs of the student, including competence in the subject, or all the subjects, that he may be called upon to teach. A group major (i.e., social studies, science, humanities), as distinct from a single-subject major (i.e., history, economics, chemistry), corresponds more closely to existing curriculum patterns in the secondary school. For the social studies teacher in training, the subject possibilities are wide, and genuine mastery of all of them is impossible in the four-year course. How much the prospective teacher may learn about Russia depends upon the offerings available in his major subjects and upon his program requirements. Within these limitations, however, opportunities exist for students planning to become teachers to work out a program, by careful selection and with the assistance of their advisors, which will include some general preparation in the Russian area.

A related problem is that of certification and assignment to teach. Again, the practices vary widely from state to state, but certification to teach social studies usually means certification to teach any subject in that category, and may be acquired on the basis of considerably less than a major in any single subject. Teachers may be certified to teach social studies with a minor in that field, which may mean no preparation in depth in any particular subject in it. School administrators regularly assign teachers to courses in accord with these certification standards and regardless of whether the teachers have had special training in the subject assigned, or in other subjects. Therefore, whether or not opportunities are provided for majoring in Russian studies in teacher education programs, there is under present procedures no necessary correlation between such special preparation and teaching assignment. A recent study of social studies teachers in the secondary schools of Kansas showed that of the 315 social studies teachers assigned to teach world history, only 151 had had any college work in modern European history, and only 27 any college work in Far Eastern history.

Opportunity for the study of Russia can nevertheless be found in the teacher-training program. In states where the department of education, as certifying agency, does not dictate specific course requirements but rather approves college programs of teacher preparation individually, institutions can explore special interests such as Russian studies. And while the professional education part of teacher-preparation programs might appear to have little connection with the problem, the contrary is true. Potentialities for the study of other cultures and social systems, whether utilized or not, exist in this part of the curriculum, for example, in the subject commonly called "Foundations

167

of Education." Courses labelled "School and Society," "Principles of Secondary Education," and so on, are often unnecessarily provincial. They could well afford to give some consideration to comparative education. This would appear especially timely in view of the current interest in Russian education. The part of the professional education curriculum devoted to materials and methods also provides fruitful possibilities. Courses concerned with the teaching of social studies, in particular, offer excellent opportunity for a presentation of ways in which comparative Russian materials might be used in class. Student teaching presents still other opportunities. Some student teachers should be encouraged to prepare and teach Russian units.

The interrelationship between the teaching of secondary-school social studies courses and other levels of the American educational system, undergraduate and graduate, needs to be stressed. Most of the teachers being prepared today go to multipurpose institutions, not to "teachers colleges." Those in charge of teacher training within liberal arts colleges could and should call upon the total resources of the institution. The scholar has the power and the responsibility to make an impact on the teacher in training. If the secondary schools are to give more attention to the study of Russia, the 1,300 or more liberal arts colleges involved in teacher training must provide prospective teachers with the necessary preparation.

In developing ways to equip teachers with some knowledge of Russian and Soviet developments, several additional problems arise. For example, in the multipurpose tax-supported institution, from which many teachers are drawn, it

168

is often difficult to identify future teachers early enough to permit the inclusion of specialized preparation in their program. Furthermore, a great many American children are being taught in small schools, although educational leaders tend to think in terms of large schools. Teaching problems are different in each case; in a small school the teacher usually has to teach in at least two fields in which he has not been trained.

A program of teacher training in Russian studies probably has its best opportunity to achieve an immediate impact on the school program through what is generally known as "in-service education." Several types are common: one is formal work for additional credit undertaken by the practicing teacher at night or in the summer; a second is the special conference, institute, or consultative use of specialists on a particular topic or problem; and a third is independent reading, travel, or participation in professional organizations of individual teachers. In all of these cases, concentration on Russian studies would enable teachers not previously prepared in this field to acquire the basis for including more attention to Russia in present courses, provided suitable teaching materials were made available. For example, the University of Michigan presented, in the summer of 1958, a special program of Russian studies. The program included an interdepartmental survey of the Soviet Union, as well as elective courses on Russia in the departments of economics, geography, history, political science, and Slavic languages and literature. An intensive Russian language program was also offered. A program of this type is of special value to teachers wishing to augment

169

their teaching effectiveness by acquiring some competence in the field of Russian studies.

Although instructional materials are designed primarily for use by students, leaders in teacher education generally agree that nothing determines the nature of the curriculum so much as the textbook. Efforts to influence the curriculum may well take textbooks as a point of departure. World history textbooks are perhaps the most relevant for the study of Russia, but their treatment of Russia and other areas is limited by traditional considerations and course requirements. Publishers must produce volumes acceptable to the educational public. At present this means that a book must not be too long, or teachers cannot carry their students through it in a single year. Furthermore, as a world history, it will need to include Mayan, for example, as well as Russian civilization. At the same time, by careful selection and by giving Russia space and attention commensurate with its importance in history and in the modern world, it should be possbile to expand and improve the treatment of Russia in such textbooks, without making less effective their presentation of world history as a whole. Other reading materials besides textbooks should also be used, however, if any substantial teaching about Russia is to result.

In the effort to introduce and develop the study of Russia in American schools, it is essential that the alternatives available respecting the curriculum be carefully considered in the light of their utility and feasibility. One is a separate course in Russian studies, taught for a semester or even a year. Another is increased emphasis on Russian studies within existing curricular patterns. In either case, the introduction of Russian studies will probably be only an opening wedge leading to greater emphasis on non-Western studies in general in the secondary-school curriculum. Teacher education programs, therefore, may follow one of two alternatives: (1) the training of a small, select group of teachers with considerable preparation on Russia for those secondary schools, probably few in number, that wish to offer special courses or programs relating to the Russian area; such teachers might be students of Russian and Soviet society, or persons who combine this with ability to teach the Russian language; (2) emphasis on providing a general knowledge of Russian culture to a large number of secondary-school teachers, few of whom would become Russian specialists.

In teacher education and in the curriculum, the introduction of materials on Communism alone is not enough; concentration on the history, society, and culture of Russia, as well as on Communism, is essential. We need to know something of the area as a whole rather than merely the ideology of its government. This broader approach would also provide a more solid basis for the study of Russia than would emphasis on the present-day foreign and domestic policies of the U.S.S.R. For such an approach, study of the Russian language provides an immediate and, at the present time, increasingly popular complementary step.

III

The furor that followed the success of the Russian space satellite program brought forth a rash of proposals for introducing more study of science and foreign languages

171

in American secondary schools. Dr. Marjorie Johnston, of the United States Office of Education, has posed the problem in this way: "We no longer live in an age in which knowledge of a foreign language can be considered more or less exclusively as either the hallmark of the literary scholar or the sign of the illiterate immigrant. Nor can it be any longer the sole domain of a handful of specialists who make their living by teaching, research, translating, or interpreting."

In the past there has been little study of the Russian language in American secondary schools, or even in American colleges, and there is an urgent need to remedy this deficiency. Considerations of national, as well as of cultural and scientific, interest suggest that Russian should be the first of the languages not previously taught to be added to the secondary-school curriculum. Several conferences of foreign-language teachers in 1958 adopted resolutions stressing the urgent need for introducing Russian in the secondary schools. Public, as distinct from professional, reaction to the proposal to teach Russian can perhaps be gauged by the enthusiastic response to televised courses of Russian language instruction at unusual hours. Soviet scientific achievements, and the novelty of studying a language few Americans know and most Americans consider exotic, set a favorable stage for introducing Russian in the secondary schools.

The annual convention of the American Association of Teachers of Slavic and East European Languages (AATSEEL) at Madison, Wisconsin, in September, 1957, organized a Committee for Promoting the Study of Russian in American High Schools. Operating on the basis of regional representation, the committee encouraged the introduction of pilot courses and cooperated in developing them. By the fall of 1958, over two hundred public and at least two dozen private secondary schools were teaching Russian. These were not all new programs. The Maine Township High School, Des Plaines, Illinois, for example, has been teaching Russian for about four years, using the traditional instructional methods based on a grammar text. In Portland, Oregon, Russian has been taught since 1944; the methods used are somewhat less traditional, and the teachers all teach other courses as well as Russian language. In some school systems (e.g., Stuyvesant, Erasmus Hall High School, and the Bronx School of Science, in the New York City system) Russian has been offered outside the regular curriculum as a special club activity. A number of private secondary schools have also been teaching Russian for some time. St. Alban's (Washington, D. C.) follows the traditional grammar-reading-conversation approach, while Choate (Wallingford, Connecticut) uses the oral-aural approach. Chatham Hall (Chatham, Virginia) has for some fifteen years offered a combined course in elementary Russian language and Russian culture.

Since 1944 the University of Minnesota High School has offered a Russian language and civilization course similar to its German, French, and Spanish language and civilization courses. When instruction in a language is introduced, lectures on the literature are added to the English class on world literature, folk songs and music by national composers are included in the music appreciation class, and folk dances become part of the physical education class.

The great variation in approach of the small number of Russian language programs among the approximately 28,-000 public and private secondary schools in the United States, and the highly selected group of students usually involved, make difficult an evaluation of their effectiveness and their suitability as general models. By and large, the most successful programs have been characterized by strong support from the administration and the community, as well as the students and teachers, by careful recruitment of qualified teachers, and by painstaking selection of materials, with well-planned syllabi.

Conferences sponsored in 1958 by the Modern Language Association and by AATSEEL on teaching Russian language did not reflect unanimity on the proper method of instruction. The oral-aural approach and the so-called traditional reading-writing-conversation approach both have strong advocates. In regard to teachers, there was a broader range of agreement that the ideal qualifications of a Russian language teacher for American secondary-school classrooms are complete oral-aural facility, thorough knowledge of the historical and cultural background of Russia, an understanding of the theory of languages, and a familiarity with classroom procedures. It is clear, however, that only a few teachers with these qualifications are now available; consequently, every effort must be made to find and prepare Russian language teachers who can quickly meet modified standards designed to ensure that reasonably competent instruction in Russian is offered.

Emergency qualification of teachers for Russian language instruction is taking place. In-service training courses for teachers are available in some areas, as in New York City. In some states, Connecticut for example, teachers have been accepted on a temporary basis, without the usual certification requirements, after meeting a test of proficiency and cultural background supervised by a competent non-state authority, in this case, Yale. During the summers teacher training courses are being offered by such institutions as Middlebury College, Columbia Teachers College, Indiana University, the University of Michigan, the University of Pennsylvania, Yale University, Brooklyn College, and the University of Minnesota.

Although such emergency measures may be able temporarily to alleviate the shortage of teachers, a large-scale growth of Russian language instruction in the secondary schools will require a systematic and long-range effort in teacher education, and a rapid expansion of Russian language study in institutions of higher education. For example, in 1956-57, of 340,000 bachelor's degrees granted, only 107 were majors in Russian; of 61,955 master's degrees, only 33 were majors in Russian; of 8,756 persons awarded doctor's degrees, 10 were Russian language specialists. These students are not the only possible source for teachers of Russian in American secondary schools, to be sure, but the figures above suggest the paucity of individuals being prepared in the customary teacher-training programs upon

175

which certification authorities draw for public school teachers.

Procedural techniques in language teaching have changed in the past twenty years by a margin not duplicated in any other subject matter, largely because of developments in the science of linguistics and the growing availability of technical aids. Although there is disagreement as to the relative merit of using native Americans to teach foreign languages, or of utilizing in American classrooms recent refugees, neither group should be automatically excluded, and both can be assisted by modern language methods and aids. Certainly there are not enough native speakers to supply the needs of the secondary schools even if they met other requirements for language teachers; at the same time the skills of the best native speakers can be made more widely available through recordings and tapes and can supplement teaching by native Americans. In addition, a number of teachers of Latin, French, German, and Spanish can be prepared, through special training programs, to teach Russian as well.

IV

Any knowledge of Russia introduced at the secondary-school level should be for purposes of general education. In some fields the secondary-school student normally expects to use the training he receives directly and immediately in his vocation. For other skills in which the secondary school offers training—mathematics, foreign languages, social studies—general rather than vocational education is the end. A general education course may serve as preparation for college work or may introduce a student to knowledge of himself and society basic to good citizenship and future intellectual and cultural growth. The study of Russia in the secondary schools should be directed toward giving the student an understanding of the concepts and principles that are basic in Russian history, society, and language. Even there, the very few students who later embark upon a career of specialization in Russian area studies would benefit by learning these subjects at the secondary-school level almost exclusively as cultural subjects designed to enhance their intellectual breadth. This means that the study of Russia does not have to be tied to their own immediate daily experience.

What we need to learn about the peoples and societies of Russia and the Communist orbit is an awareness of the ways in which their problems, traditions, and points of view compare with ours. It is now generally recognized that the Soviet Union and its allies represent a major force in world affairs, and that the maintenance of peace in an era of vigorous competition will call for skill and understanding. Apart from contributing to a comprehension of the essential features of Russian society, the study of an important foreign area such as this should also contribute to a deeper appreciation of the American way of life. Such consideration of one's own society in comparison with other cultures is vital to the educational process and should be an important by-product of foreign area study.

Given the time required for learning, no program is going to provide over night any general remedy for our

177

present problem of inadequate knowledge of non-Western languages, history, institutions, and culture. "Crash" programs can meet the irreducible demand by concentrating on a few people and training them without regard to the cost. But public education, which is relatively inflexible, cannot be expected to convert en masse to any "crash" program. If Russian and other non-Western studies are to receive the serious attention in secondary education which the role of the United States in international affairs requires, this goal cannot be best achieved in the long run by scissors-and-paste curriculum-making, inserting a unit here or an elective for the academically talented there. We must instead divide the available time in such a way as to give due weight to these studies in relation to more traditional subject matter. Such a division, rather than interlarding special courses whenever their contemporary importance strikes us, will commit us to a long-range approach. One means of achieving this may be through broader use of a comparative and illustrative approach in the social studies units now offered to all, taught by teachers with some preparation in Russian studies, and expanded in special units designed to emphasize the integral role of foreign-area studies in any general education program.

At present it does not appear feasible to attempt to coordinate language study with area study in the secondary-school curriculum. This is especially true if language study is looked upon as primarily useful for those going on to college. In any event, not more than 14 per cent of those enrolled in secondary schools take any foreign language at all (in the state of Indiana, which is not atypical, the figure is nearer 5 per cent), even though over 30 per cent of college-age young people enter colleges.

Our objective for the next five years might well be to double the *percentage* of those enrolled in secondary schools who study a foreign language. Without affecting the *number* of those now taking French and Spanish, this would permit more adequate attention to other languages of great significance for the twentieth-century world. Then, instead of 92 per cent of those who study a foreign language in secondary school at all studying Spanish and French, a significant proportion of the increased total number of language students would be studying Russian. There would still be some three-quarters of a million secondary-school enrollments in Spanish and French, but we should be adding to them a substantial enrollment in Russian and in other languages now neglected. There would still be only some 30 per cent of secondary-school students in any foreign-language program, but an effort should be made to include all those who are likely to continue formal study beyond the twelfth grade.

Effective planning for the future requires that the possible, as well as the desirable, be taken into account. With this in mind, what, then, are the practical steps that can be taken to encourage greater attention to Russia in secondary education, with the eventual goal of having every secondary-school graduate know some basic information about Russia and the Communist system?

In considering curricular problems, certain basic assumptions must be taken into account. The most important is, that in taking measures to include more attention to Russia

179

and other non-Western areas, major emphasis should be on alterations within the existing course structure rather than on the addition of special area courses. The former is the more feasible approach and also ensures reaching the largest number of students. Social studies are already a part of all programs, and through present social studies a wide cross-section of the secondary-school population can be informed about Russia. Since these courses are already crowded with subject matter, some re-allocation of the time devoted to various topics and greater stress on comparative and illustrative material relating to Russia will be necessary. The goal should be a reconsideration of content in the social studies program to provide an emphasis on Russia and other non-Western areas proportionate to their importance in the modern world, and to give the study of these areas an organic connection with the general education program.

Special projects like that in Russian history at the University of Wisconsin High School are excellent in that they stand on their own merits as study in a foreign area. The difficulty is that they reach only a fraction of those in social studies programs and must compete for attention with other subjects aimed at the same fraction. They are also difficult to prepare and arrange and are not likely to be widely adopted in the immediate future. They are nevertheless of great value in encouraging interest in Russian studies and as experimental pilot programs which may show the way to a number of other schools.

It is apparent that curriculum modification can be effective only if there is close and continuing cooperation among scholars, teachers, and secondary-school administrators. Another assumption is that in handling Russian materials in the curriculum a broad fields approach, including sociology, economics, anthropology, and other disciplines, should be adopted.

A final postulate is the necessity for a carefully planned expansion of instruction in the Russian language as a complement to study of the languages traditionally taught in secondary schools. Where possible, the teaching of Russian should be initiated in the elementary schools as well. At whatever level it is taught, a minimum of two years' study of Russian should be offered, and in most cases it would be desirable for secondary schools to offer a three or four-year sequence in Russian.

V

A vital problem in teaching about Russia in the secondary schools is how to present the findings of American and other Western research in such a way as to give students a mature and balanced understanding of a very different historical experience and way of life. The judicious adaptation of these findings to secondary-school teaching will require further study and experimentation, and this paper can touch only briefly on some of the problems involved.

A basic general premise is that Russia—not merely the Soviet Union—is the topic. The origins of Russian institutions must be studied, and elements of continuity and change in Tsarist and Soviet development should be examined.

As noted above, much material on Russia can be initially introduced into existing social studies courses, as well as through special courses on the area. For example, fundamental to an understanding of Russia is a knowledge of its geography. Geography courses should therefore embrace not only location identification relating to Russia and an awareness of its main physical and climatological features, but also an appreciation of the influence of Russian geography on history and foreign policy, including the growth of the Russian empire. Important also is a recognition of the many nationalities and language families embraced in the area of the Soviet Union.

In world history courses, the presentation of Russian history should certainly be more than chronologically-arranged facts about strange and distant peoples. To integrate Russian history with the whole of a pupil's education, the question of Russian origins and the relation of Russia to Europe should be raised. In its origins Russia was a fusion of Germanic tribal custom and Greek Christianity imposed on a Slavic population. Medieval Western civilization similarly grew out of the fusion of Germanic peoples and Latin Christianity. Students should also be reminded, in this age of Soviet anticlericalism, that Russia was a great Christian country throughout the centuries which witnessed the rise of the major Western European nation states. Consequently, due attention should be devoted to the Byzantine culture area and its great legacy, the Orthodox Church, and Russia should be identified as a principal heir of the Eastern Roman Empire.

A sound interpretation of Russian history should include

an examination of whether we should regard Russia as part of the Western world or not. Students should be made aware of the fact that in the twelfth century Russia and Western Europe had much in common, but that the former did not experience the great events of the following centuries which affected Western Europe so greatly, e.g., the Renaissance and the Reformation. During the expansion of Western civilization other parts of the world borrowed, or were forced to adopt, aspects of Western civilization. Both America and Russia can be seen as extensions of Europe, America becoming a new center of Western civilization, Russia learning from Europe but holding to its own messianic vision, adapting what it learned in order to use the knowledge in combating European hegemony, and on occasion treating Europe as a corrupt deviant in the development of civilization. The thesis that Russia will replace Europe as the center of civilization has a long tradition in Russian history and should be one of the insights into Russian development acquired from a Russian-studies program.

Students should learn about the institutions of serfdom and autocracy in Russia and should recognize that the pattern of modernization in Russia was largely inspired by the West. This is true even of Marxism, which was born in the West, imported by Russia, and altered into its present Soviet manifestation. Conversely, it is useful to show the contributions that the great flowering of Russian culture in the nineteenth and early twentieth centuries made to Western literature, music, and other arts.

The periodization of Russian history can be used to

illustrate some important universal principles in the history of other modern societies. The significance of 1861 as a turning point in Russian history is well recognized. What should be equally recognized is the continuity between pre- and post-1861 peasant life. As is always true in any major upheaval, the characteristics of the pre-revolutionary organization of society that are preserved may be quite as important as those which are changed. The same, in differing degree, is true of the problem of 1917 as a turning point in Russian history.

Ideally, study of Communism and the Soviet system in courses on problems of democracy should be based on a prior acquaintance with Russia's past gained in world history courses. Attention should be given to the theory of Communism as developed by Marx and to the alterations it has undergone in the face of changing conditions and in practice. The existence of a number of varieties of Communism should also be noted, as well as the ways these differ from each other and from the theory. In the study of Soviet foreign policy, it is important that students recognize that Communist plans to dominate the world are not all military in nature, and that political and economic tactics form an important part of Communist strategy.

In broad outline, students should learn about the growth of Soviet industrial, economic, and technological power, as well as the very heavy human and material costs of this achievement. The significance of Soviet methods of economic development for the underdeveloped nations of Asia and Africa should also be pointed out. In addition, so far as this is possible at the secondary-school level, the Soviet system could be used to illustrate the relationship between economic development and political and social structure in modernizing society.

In short, it is a question of understanding the problems and nature of a society and way of life that are very different from ours in many respects. Soviet society is a closed society and offers to the student an example of a totalitarian regime embracing the family, the school system, and art and culture, as well as political and economic life. Like all societies it is constantly changing, but in whatever direction it may evolve it represents a continuing force in international relations about which all Americans should be informed and concerned.

American history provides a less effective vehicle for references to Russia except for the most recent period, although there are a number of historical examples of American-Russian relations in earlier years. There is the possibility as well of developing analogies between the expansion of the American frontier and Russian expansion into Siberia, and between American slavery and Russian serfdom, as well as emphasizing comparisons in matters relating to civil liberties, free enterprise, and living standards. American history courses also present the opportunity to consider lessons which may be learned from Western intervention in Russia, and an evaluation of the United States image of the Soviet Union.

In world literature courses some attention may well be devoted to popular Russian authors of the nineteenth century, such as Tolstoy and Chekhov, and to a few Soviet writers. In activities inside or outside the classroom relating to music, drama, and the dance, Russian and Soviet contributions to these art forms could readily be made clear.

VI

In conclusion, attention should be drawn to the related questions of training teachers and of providing materials and other assistance to schools that wish to develop the teaching of Russia and of other non-Western areas. An essential step is the education of teachers interested in and equipped to teach about these areas. In the pre-service preparation of teachers at all levels, there should be continuing emphasis on the general education and liberal arts approaches, and such preparation should permit of both breadth and depth. Within this broader framework, opportunities should be provided, wherever possible, for teachers to include a major or minor in area studies in their pre-service preparation. If this is to be done, institutions preparing teachers will have to make available more offerings in the social sciences relating to the Russian area. These approaches to the pre-service preparation of teachers in Russian studies should benefit from efforts in teacher education to place expanded emphasis on subject-matter courses.

A number of important ways exist for encouraging and assisting the study of Russia by teachers who have already been trained. A most useful aid would be selected and annotated book lists on the Russian area for teachers and school librarians. Such lists could be prepared by specialists in Russian studies in consultation with social studies teachers in the secondary schools. Also of great value would be short studies for the teacher or the student dealing with various aspects of Russian affairs—for example, brief treatments of Soviet economic growth and organization, of the origins of Bolshevism and the revolutions of 1917, of Soviet social structure, of major problems in Russian and Soviet foreign policy. Studies of this type should also be prepared through the cooperative efforts of specialists in the field and secondary-school teachers and administrators. A number of such studies might later be combined and issued in book form. Other helpful materials for teachers would be various audio-visual aids, ranging from television programs and films to slides and film strips. The latter could often be prepared from photographs or movies taken by recent visitors to Russia. A list of audio-visual devices and of their availability might usefully accompany the book lists mentioned above when they are circulated to schools and teachers.

A substantial contribution to the stimulation of institutional and teacher interest and to the in-service preparation of teachers could be made through the establishment of regional or state consulting services in Russian studies. Such services should be supervised and staffed by area specialists, in conjunction with schools and departments of education. Included in the services made available might be the preparation and distribution of the materials discussed in the preceding paragraph, guidance on problems of curriculum and content for school administrators and teachers anxious to initiate instruction in the Russian language or area, and frequent visits to and close cooperation with schools and teachers in the region. Direct contact with teachers in their schools and occasionally with students would be very desirable, although this would require a large amount of the university teachers' time.

A most important step would be the offering of special summer programs on Russia for secondary-school teachers. These might take the form of an institute or workshop bringing together teachers who had developed resource units. Such brief efforts, whether in the summer or during the course of the school year, are most effective, however, when they are combined with a program of regular course offerings relating to the Russian area. It is essential, therefore, that universities with resources in Russian studies develop and offer substantive programs in the Russian language and the area designed to meet the needs and objectives of secondary-school teachers.

To ensure continuing attention to the problem of developing the study of Russia in American secondary education and to promote the necessary cooperation in this effort between scholars in Russian studies and secondary-school teachers and administrators, a national joint committee of representatives of the two groups should be established. The functions of this committee would be to consider immediate and long-range projects and the needs and desires of the schools and teachers, and to act as a clearinghouse of information on the subject. It could provide limited guidance and an indication of what others interested in the problem were doing.

Such a committee should be small, but knowledgeable about personnel, sources of financial support, and other resources. Its long-run goal would be to help with conferences, advise textbook authors and publishers, counsel on the education of teachers, assist in experimentation at the local level, and make other suggestions upon request. In short, its role would be one of guiding and servicing the growing number of scholars, teachers, and administrators who are convinced that some acquaintance with Russia, as well as with other non-Western areas, should become an integral and accepted part of the preparation of almost every secondary-school student.

DATE DUE

PRINTED IN U.S.A.